CW00358077

# It's another Quality Book from CGP

This book is for anyone doing Edexcel Modular Science.

Whatever subject you're doing it's the same
old story — there are lots of facts and you've just got
to learn them. Edexcel Modular Science is no different.

The good news however is that this CGP book delivers
the hard cold facts as clearly as possible.

It's also got some daft bits in to try and make the whole
experience at least vaguely entertaining for you.

---

Higher

Some of the material is only needed at Higher level.
We've stuck this stuff in blue boxes (like this one) so it's easy to find in the book.

Higher

---

# What CGP is all about

Our sole aim here at CGP is to produce the highest quality
books — carefully written, immaculately presented and
dangerously close to being funny.

Then we work our socks off to get them out to you
— at the cheapest possible prices.

# Book 2     Contents

# Book 2

# Contents

Published by Coordination Group Publications Ltd
Illustrations by:   Sandy Gardner   e-mail: illustrations@sandygardner.co.uk
and Bowser, Colorado USA

Additional illustrations by CGP

Consultant Editor: Paddy Gannon

Updated by:
Matthew Ball
Chris Bates
Gemma Hallam
Tim Major
Tessa Moulton
Andy Park
Philip Robson
Julie Schofield

ISBN 1 84146 940 8

Groovy Website:   www.cgpbooks.co.uk

Proofreading by:
Dr David Worthington
Mrs Eileen Worthington

Printed by Elanders Hindson, Newcastle upon Tyne.
Clipart sources: CorelDRAW and VECTOR.

Text, design, layout and original illustrations © Coordination Group Publications Ltd
All rights reserved.  Terrible things will happen if you nick our stuff.

# Cells

*Action in Leaves*

## Plant Cells and Animal Cells Have Their Differences

You need to be able to draw these two cells <u>with all the details</u> for each.

### Animal Cell

**FOUR THINGS THEY BOTH HAVE IN COMMON:**

1) <u>NUCLEUS</u> contains genetic material that controls what the cell <u>does</u>.

2) <u>CYTOPLASM</u> contains enzymes that <u>speed up</u> biological reactions.

3) <u>CELL MEMBRANE</u> holds the cell together and controls what goes <u>in</u> and <u>out</u>.

4) <u>MITOCHONDRIA</u> turn glucose and oxygen into <u>energy</u>.

### Plant Cell

**EXTRAS THAT ONLY PLANT CELLS HAVE:**

1) <u>RIGID CELL WALL</u> made of <u>cellulose</u>, gives support for the cell.

2) <u>VACUOLE</u> contains <u>cell sap</u>, a weak solution of sugar and salts.

3) <u>CHLOROPLASTS</u> containing <u>chlorophyll</u> for <u>photosynthesis</u>. *Found in the green parts of plants.*

## Different Bits of a Plant do Different Jobs

### 1) Flower

This allows the plant to <u>pollinate</u> and <u>reproduce</u>.

### 2) Leaf

It produces <u>food</u> for the plant. I'll say it again, listen....
<u>The leaf produces all the food that the plant needs</u>.

*Plants do not take food from the soil. Plants make <u>all their own food</u> in their leaves using <u>photosynthesis</u>.*

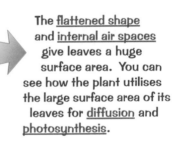

The <u>flattened shape</u> and <u>internal air spaces</u> give leaves a huge surface area. You can see how the plant utilises the large surface area of its leaves for <u>diffusion</u> and <u>photosynthesis</u>.

### 3) Stem

1) This holds the plant <u>upright</u>.
2) Also, <u>water</u> and <u>food</u> travel <u>up and down</u> the stem.

### 4) Root hairs

These give <u>a big surface area</u> to <u>absorb</u> <u>water</u> and <u>ions</u> from the soil.

### 5) Root

1) Its main job is <u>anchorage</u>.
2) It also takes in <u>water</u> and a few <u>mineral ions</u> from the soil. But mostly just water.
<u>REMEMBER, plants do not take 'food' in from the soil</u>.

## The Big Idea is to LEARN All That...

Everything on this page is there to be <u>learnt</u> because it's very likely to come up in your Exams. This is pretty basic stuff, but it can still catch you out if you don't learn it properly. For example: "What is the main function of the root?". Too many people answer that with "Taking food in from the soil" — Eeek!

Action in Leaves

# Photosynthesis

## Photosynthesis Produces Glucose from Sunlight

1) <u>Photosynthesis</u> is the process that produces '<u>food</u>' in plants. The 'food' it produces is <u>glucose</u>.
2) Photosynthesis takes place in the <u>leaves</u> of all <u>green plants</u> — this is what leaves are for.
3) Photosynthesis uses energy from the Sun. Leaves are <u>thin</u> and <u>flat</u> to provide a <u>big surface area</u> to catch <u>lots</u> of sunlight.

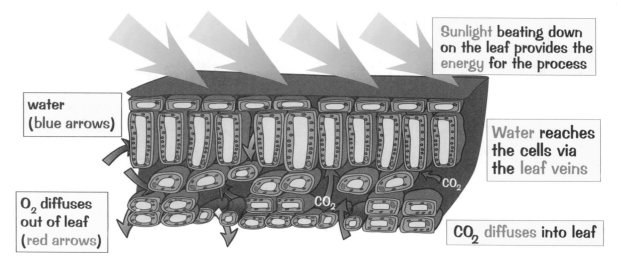

Sunlight beating down on the leaf provides the energy for the process

water (blue arrows)

Water reaches the cells via the leaf veins

O$_2$ diffuses out of leaf (red arrows)

CO$_2$ diffuses into leaf

## Learn the Equation for Photosynthesis:

$$\text{Carbon dioxide} + \text{Water} \xrightarrow[\text{chlorophyll}]{\text{LIGHT ENERGY}} \text{glucose} + \text{oxygen}$$

## Four Things are Needed for Photosynthesis to Happen:

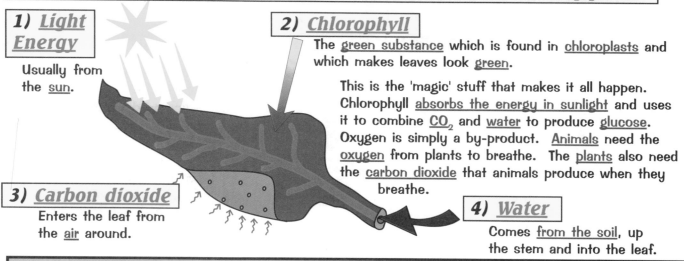

### 1) Light Energy

Usually from the <u>sun</u>.

### 2) Chlorophyll

The <u>green substance</u> which is found in <u>chloroplasts</u> and which makes leaves look <u>green</u>.

This is the 'magic' stuff that makes it all happen. Chlorophyll <u>absorbs the energy in sunlight</u> and uses it to combine <u>CO$_2$</u> and <u>water</u> to produce <u>glucose</u>. Oxygen is simply a by-product. <u>Animals</u> need the <u>oxygen</u> from plants to breathe. The <u>plants</u> also need the <u>carbon dioxide</u> that animals produce when they breathe.

### 3) Carbon dioxide

Enters the leaf from the <u>air</u> around.

### 4) Water

Comes <u>from the soil</u>, up the stem and into the leaf.

## Live and Learn...

What you've got to do now is learn <u>everything</u> on this page. Photosynthesis is a "dead cert" for the Exams. On this page you've got two diagrams, three points about photosynthesis and the equation, and then the four necessary conditions. Just <u>keep learning them</u> until you can <u>cover the page</u> and write them all down <u>from memory</u>. Only then will you really <u>know it all</u>.

# Diffusion

Action in Leaves

## Don't be put off by the fancy word

"Diffusion" is really simple. It's just the gradual movement of particles from places where there are lots of them to places where there are fewer of them.

That's all it is — it's just the natural tendency for stuff to spread out.

Unfortunately you also have to learn the fancy way of saying the same thing, which is this:

**DIFFUSION is the PASSIVE MOVEMENT OF PARTICLES from an area of HIGH CONCENTRATION to an area of LOW CONCENTRATION**

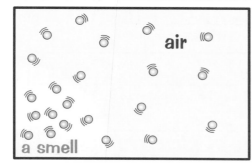
a smell / air

smell diffused in the air

## Diffusion of Gases in Leaves is vital for Photosynthesis

The simplest type of diffusion is where different gases diffuse through each other, like when a weird smell spreads out through the air in a room. Diffusion of gases also happens in leaves and they'll very likely put it in your Exam. So learn it now:

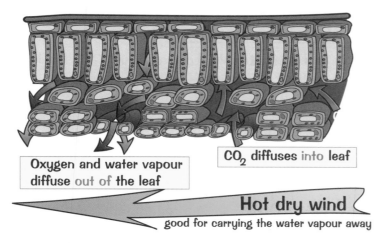

Oxygen and water vapour diffuse out of the leaf

$CO_2$ diffuses into leaf

Hot dry wind
good for carrying the water vapour away

For photosynthesis to happen, carbon dioxide gas has to get inside the leaves.
It does this by diffusion through the tiny little holes under the leaf called stomata.

At the same time water vapour and oxygen diffuse out through the same tiny little holes.

The water vapour escapes by diffusion because there's a lot of it inside the leaf and less of it in the air outside. This diffusion causes transpiration and it goes quicker when the air around the leaf is kept dry — ie. transpiration is quickest in hot, dry, windy conditions — and don't you forget it!

## Diffusion — silent but deadly...

Yeah sure it's a pretty book but actually the big idea is to learn all the stuff that's in it.
So learn this page until you can answer these questions without having to look back:

1) Write down the fancy definition for diffusion, and then say what it means in your own words.
2) Draw the cross-section of the leaf with arrows to show which way the three gases diffuse.
3) What weather conditions make the diffusion of water vapour out of the leaf go fastest?

# The Rate of Photosynthesis

*Action in Leaves*

The <u>rate</u> of <u>photosynthesis</u> is affected by <u>three factors</u>:

## 1) THE AMOUNT OF LIGHT

The <u>chlorophyll</u> uses <u>light energy</u> to perform photosynthesis. It can only do it as fast as the light energy is arriving. Chlorophyll actually only absorbs the <u>red</u> and <u>blue</u> ends of the <u>visible light</u> <u>spectrum</u>, but not the <u>green light</u> in the middle, which is <u>reflected</u> back. This is why the plant looks green.

## 2) THE AMOUNT OF CARBON DIOXIDE

<u>$CO_2$</u> and <u>water</u> are the <u>raw materials</u>. Water is never really in short supply in a plant but only <u>0.03%</u> of the air around is $CO_2$ so it's actually <u>pretty scarce</u> as far as plants are concerned.

## 3) THE TEMPERATURE

<u>Chlorophyll</u> is like an <u>enzyme</u> in that it works best when it's <u>warm but not too hot</u>. The rate of photosynthesis depends on how 'happy' the chlorophyll is: WARM but not too hot.

## Three Important Graphs For Rate of Photosynthesis

At any given time one or other of the above <u>three factors</u> will be the <u>limiting factor</u> which is keeping the photosynthesis <u>down</u> at the rate it is.

### 1) Not Enough LIGHT Slows Down the Rate of Photosynthesis

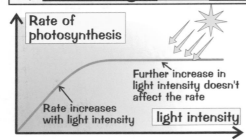

Rate of photosynthesis

Further increase in light intensity doesn't affect the rate

Rate increases with light intensity

light intensity

1) As the <u>light level</u> is raised, the rate of photosynthesis <u>increases steadily</u> but only up to a <u>certain point</u>.

2) Beyond that, it won't make any <u>difference</u> because then it'll be either the <u>temperature</u> or the <u>$CO_2$</u> level which is the limiting factor.

### 2) Too Little CARBON DIOXIDE also Slows it Down

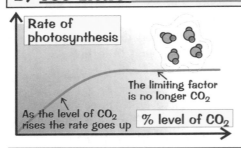

Rate of photosynthesis

The limiting factor is no longer $CO_2$

As the level of $CO_2$ rises the rate goes up

% level of $CO_2$

1) As with light intensity the amount of <u>$CO_2$</u> will only increase the rate of photosynthesis up to a point. After this the graph <u>flattens out</u> showing that $CO_2$ is no longer the <u>limiting factor</u>.

2) As long as <u>light</u> and <u>$CO_2$</u> are in plentiful supply then the factor limiting photosynthesis must be <u>temperature</u>.

### 3) The TEMPERATURE has to be Just Right

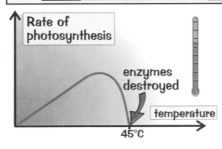

Rate of photosynthesis

enzymes destroyed

temperature

45°C

1) Note that you can't really have <u>too much</u> light or $CO_2$. The <u>temperature</u> however must <u>not</u> get too high or it <u>destroys</u> the chlorophyll.

2) This happens at about 45°C (which is pretty hot for outdoors, though greenhouses can get that hot if you're not careful).

3) <u>Usually</u>, though, if the temperature is the <u>limiting factor</u> it's because it's <u>too low</u>, and things need warming up a bit.

## Revision — life isn't all fun and sunshine...

There are three limiting factors, a graph for each and an explanation of why the graphs level off or stop abruptly. <u>Cover the page</u> and practise <u>recalling all these details</u>, until you can do it.

# How Plants Use The Glucose

 **For** *Respiration*

1) Plants manufacture <u>glucose</u> in their <u>leaves</u>.
2) They then use some of the glucose initially for <u>respiration</u>.
3) This <u>releases energy</u> which enables them to <u>convert</u> the rest of the glucose into various <u>other useful substances</u> which they can use to <u>build new cells</u> and <u>grow</u>.
4) To produce some of these substances they also need to <u>gather</u> a few <u>minerals</u> from the soil.

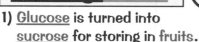 ## *Making* Fruits

1) <u>Glucose</u> is turned into <u>sucrose</u> for storing in <u>fruits</u>.
2) Fruits deliberately <u>taste nice</u> so that animals will eat them and so <u>spread the seeds</u> all over the place.

 ## *Stored in* Seeds

1) <u>Glucose</u> is turned into <u>lipids</u> (fats and oils) for storing in <u>seeds</u>.
2) <u>Sunflower seeds</u>, for example, contain a lot of oil — we get <u>cooking oil</u> and <u>margarine</u> from them.

 ## **For** *Transport*

The <u>energy</u> from <u>glucose</u> is also needed to <u>transport substances</u> around the plant and for <u>active uptake</u> of <u>minerals</u> in the roots.

 ## *Making* Cell Walls

<u>Glucose</u> is converted into <u>cellulose</u> for making <u>cell walls</u>, especially in a rapidly growing plant.

 ## *Making* Proteins

<u>Glucose</u> is combined with <u>nitrates</u> (collected from the soil) to make <u>amino acids</u>, which are then made into <u>proteins</u>.

 ## *Stored* **as Starch**

<u>Glucose</u> is turned into <u>starch</u> and <u>stored</u> in roots, stems and leaves, ready for use when photosynthesis isn't happening, like in the <u>winter</u>.

Glucose as <u>starch</u> is <u>insoluble</u> which makes it much <u>better</u> for <u>storing</u>, because it doesn't bloat the storage cells by <u>osmosis</u> like glucose would.

<u>Potato and carrot plants</u> store a lot of starch in their roots over the winter to enable a new plant to grow from it the following spring. We eat the swollen roots!

## "Sugar it", that's what I say...

There are seven things that plants do with glucose. Can you spot them? If so, <u>learn them</u>, <u>cover the page</u>, and then display your new-found knowledge. In other words, sketch out the diagram and <u>scribble down</u> the seven ways that plants use glucose, including all the extra details.

# Transport Systems in Plants

Action in Leaves

Plants need to transport various things around inside themselves. They have tubes for it.

## Phloem and Xylem Vessels Transport Different Things

1) Flowering plants have two separate sets of tubes for transporting stuff around the plant.
2) Both sets of tubes go to every part of the plant, but they are totally separate.
3) They usually run alongside each other.

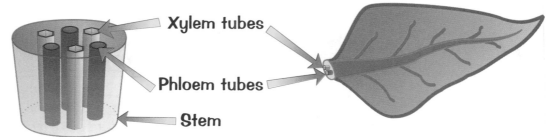

Xylem tubes

Phloem tubes

Stem

### Phloem Tubes transport Food

1) Made of living cells with perforated end-plates to allow stuff to flow through.
2) They transport food made in the leaves to all other parts of the plant, in both directions.
3) They carry sugars, fats, proteins etc to growing regions in shoot tips and root tips and to/from storage organs in the roots.

Water and food

### Xylem Tubes take water UP

1) Made of dead cells joined end to end with no end walls between them.
2) The side walls are strong and stiff and contain lignin. This gives the plant support.
3) They carry water and minerals from the roots up to the leaves in the transpiration stream.

Water and minerals

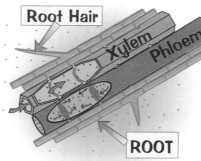

Root Hair

Xylem

Phloem

ROOT

### The Phloem and Xylem extend into the Roots

1) The phloem carries substances down to the roots for growth or for storage and may later carry them back up again.
2) The xylem carries water and minerals (which are taken in by the roots) up to the stem and into the leaves.

## Well, that seems to be about the top and bottom of it...

This is an easy page. There are important differences between xylem and phloem tubes. Make sure you know all the numbered points on this page, and the diagrams. Then cover the page and scribble it all down with detailed sketches of the diagrams. Then do it again, until you get it all.

# Minerals For Healthy Growth

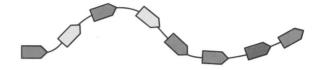

*Action in Roots*

For <u>healthy growth</u> plants need these three really important mineral ions
which they can only obtain from the <u>soil</u> through their <u>roots</u>:

## The <u>Three</u> Essential <u>Minerals</u>

### 1) <u>Nitrates</u>

— for making <u>amino acids</u> and for the
"<u>synthesis</u>" (making) of <u>proteins</u>.

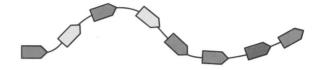

### 2) <u>Phosphates</u>

### 3) <u>Potassium</u>

— helps the <u>enzymes</u> involved in
<u>photosynthesis</u> and <u>respiration</u> to work.

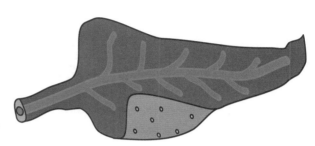

### <u>Magnesium</u> is also needed in <u>Small Amounts</u>

The three main minerals are needed in fairly large amounts, but there are other elements which
are needed in much smaller amounts. <u>MAGNESIUM</u> is pretty important, as it's required for
making <u>CHLOROPHYLL</u>, which is pretty important to plants, in case you didn't know.

## <u>Lack</u> of These Nutrients Causes <u>Deficiency Symptoms</u>:

### 1) <u>Lack of Nitrates</u>

— <u>Stunted growth</u> and <u>yellow older leaves</u>.

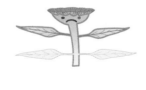

### 2) <u>Lack of Phosphates</u>

— <u>Poor root growth</u> and <u>purple younger leaves</u>.

### 3) <u>Lack of Potassium</u>

— <u>Yellow leaves</u> with <u>dead spots</u>.

## <u>Just relax and soak up the information...</u>

Very straightforward learning here. Two nice big clear sections with all the important bits
highlighted in colour as usual. You should be able to <u>cover this page</u> and <u>scribble</u> virtually the
whole thing down again with very little bother. <u>Learn and enjoy</u>.

# Active Transport

*Action in Roots*

Sometimes substances need to be absorbed <u>against</u> the concentration gradient ie: from a lower to a higher concentration. This process is lovingly referred to as ACTIVE TRANSPORT.

## *Normal <u>Diffusion</u> <u>Doesn't Work in the</u> <u>Roots</u>*

1) The cells on plant roots grow into long "<u>hairs</u>" which stick out into the soil.

2) <u>Water</u> is taken in almost entirely at the root hairs.

3) <u>Minerals</u> are also taken in at the root hairs.

4) Being long gives each hair a <u>big surface area</u> for absorbing <u>water and minerals</u> from the soil.

5) However this uptake of <u>minerals</u> is against the concentration gradient — the concentration of minerals is <u>higher</u> in the <u>root hair</u> cell than in the <u>soil</u> around it.

6) So normal diffusion <u>doesn't</u> explain how minerals are taken up into the root hair cell.

7) They should go <u>the other way</u> if they followed the rules of diffusion. This is why plants need "<u>active transport</u>" to make it happen.

The mineral concentration is higher in the root...

...than in the soil.

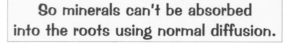

So minerals can't be absorbed into the roots using normal diffusion.

## *<u>Root Hair Cells</u> <u>take in</u> <u>Minerals</u> <u>using</u> <u>Active Transport</u>*

As shown above it is <u>impossible</u> for the <u>normal rules of diffusion</u> to apply to plant roots. They use a method called <u>active transport</u> to defy the concentration gradient. It's just a big picture and some words here so <u>no excuse</u> for not learning it.

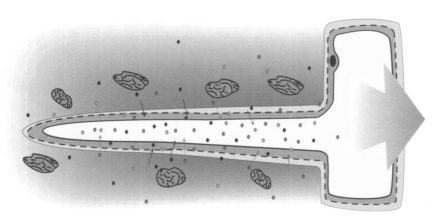

1) Active transport allows the plant to absorb minerals <u>against</u> the concentration gradient. This is essential for its growth.

2) Active transport needs energy from <u>respiration</u> to make it work.

3) Active transport also happens in <u>humans</u>, in taking glucose from the <u>gut</u> and <u>kidney tubules</u>.

## *Plants — they work hard, you know...*

Plants can't laze around relying on diffusion to get their mineral goodies. They have to <u>work</u> against the concentration gradient. That's all <u>active transport</u> is. There's nothing weird or confusing about it. All you have to do is <u>learn it</u>.

# Osmosis

## Osmosis is a Special Case of Diffusion, that's all

> OSMOSIS is the movement of water molecules across a partially permeable membrane from a region of HIGH WATER CONCENTRATION to a region of LOW WATER CONCENTRATION.

1) A selectively permeable membrane (also known as a partially permeable membrane) is just one with really small holes in it. So small, in fact, that only water molecules can pass through them, and bigger molecules like glucose can't.

2) Visking tubing is a partially permeable membrane that you should learn the name of. It's also called dialysis tubing because it's used in kidney dialysis machines.

3) The water molecules actually pass both ways through the membrane in a two-way traffic.

4) But because there are more on one side than the other there's a steady net flow into the region with fewer water molecules, ie: into the stronger solution (of glucose).

5) This causes the glucose-rich region to fill up with water. The water acts like it's trying to dilute it, so as to "even up" the concentration either side of the membrane.

6) OSMOSIS makes plant cells swell up if they're surrounded by weak solution and they become TURGID. This is real useful for giving support to green plant tissue and for opening stomatal guard cells.

7) Animal cells don't have a cell wall and can easily burst if put into pure water because they take in so much water by osmosis.

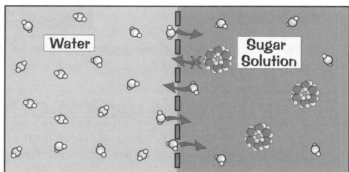

Net movement of water molecules

Animal cell bursting

## Turgor Pressure Supports Plant Tissues

When a plant is well watered, all its cells draw water into themselves by osmosis and become turgid.

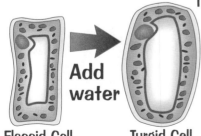

Flaccid Cell   Add water   Turgid Cell

1) When plants have enough water, the contents of the cell start to push against the cell wall, kind of like a balloon in a shoebox, and thereby give support to the plant tissues.

2) Leaves are entirely supported by this turgor pressure.

3) We know this because if there's no water in the soil, a plant starts to wilt and the leaves droop. This is because the cells start to lose water and thus lose their turgor pressure.

## Revision by Osmosis — you wish...

Osmosis can be kind of confusing if you don't get to the bottom of it. In normal diffusion, glucose molecules move, but with small enough holes they can't. That's when only water moves through the membrane, and then it's called osmosis. Easy peasy, I'd say. Learn the definition of osmosis off by heart. Learn about turgor pressure as well — it's osmosis in action.

# The Transpiration Stream

*Control Of Plant Activity*

Transpiration — it's just like drying the washing... read on and learn.

## Stomata are Pores which Open and Close Automatically

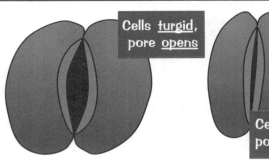 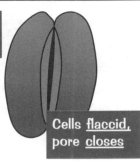

Cells turgid, pore opens

Cells flaccid, pore closes

1) Stomata close automatically when supplies of water from the roots start to dry up.

2) The guard cells control this. When water is scarce, they become flaccid, and they change shape, which closes the stomatal pores. (Limiting water loss is especially important in younger plants as water pressure is their main method of support.)

3) Closing the stomatal pores prevents any more water being lost, but also stops $CO_2$ getting in, so the photosynthesis stops as well.

## Transpiration is the loss of water from the Plant

1) It's caused by the evaporation of water from inside the leaves. Most of the action involves stomata.

2) This creates a slight shortage of water in the leaf, which draws more water up from the rest of the plant, which in turn draws more up from the roots.

3) It has two beneficial effects:
   a) it transports vital minerals from the soil into the roots and then all around the plant,
   b) it cools the plant.

water evaporates from the leaves

water soaks into the roots

### Four factors which affect it

The rate of transpiration is affected by four things:

1) Amount of light,
2) Temperature,
3) Amount of air movement,
4) Humidity of the surrounding air.

It's surely obvious that the biggest rate of transpiration occurs in hot, dry, windy, sunny conditions, ie. perfect clothes-drying weather.

By contrast a cool, cloudy, muggy, miserable day with no wind will produce minimum transpiration.

## Green stomata chutney — tasty...

There's a lot of information on this page. You could try learning the numbered points, but you'll find a better plan is to do a mini-essay on transpiration, and write down everything you can think of. Then look back to see what you've forgotten. Then do it again till you get it all.

# Growth Hormones in Plants

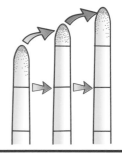

Plant Hormones

## Auxins are Plant Growth Hormones

1) Auxins are hormones which control growth at the tips of shoots and roots.
2) Auxin is produced in the tips and diffuses backwards to stimulate the cell elongation process which occurs in the cells just behind the tips.
3) If the tip of a shoot is removed, no auxin will be available and the shoot may stop growing.

## Auxins Change The Direction of Root and Shoot Growth

You'll note below that extra auxin promotes growth in the shoot but actually inhibits growth in the root — but this produces the desired result in both cases.

## 1) Shoots bend towards the light

1) When a shoot tip is exposed to light, it provides more auxin on the side that is in the shade than the side which is in the light.
2) This causes the shoot to grow faster on the shaded side and it bends towards the light.

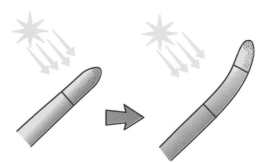

## 2) Shoots bend away from Gravity

1) When a shoot finds itself growing sideways, gravity produces an unequal distribution of auxin in the tip, with more auxin on the lower side.
2) This causes the lower side to grow faster, and the shoot bends upwards.

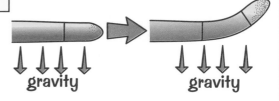

## 3) Roots bend towards Gravity

1) A root growing sideways will experience the same redistribution of auxin to the lower side.
2) But in a root the extra auxin actually inhibits growth, causing it to bend downwards instead.

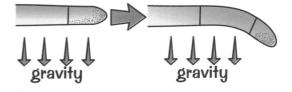

## 4) Roots bend towards Moisture

1) An uneven degree of moisture either side of a root will cause more auxin to appear on the side with more moisture.
2) This inhibits growth on that side, causing the root to grow in that direction, towards the moisture.

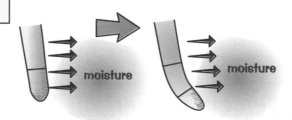

## Just a few tips for your revision...

An easy page to learn. Just three points on auxins, together with a diagram, and then four ways that shoots and roots change direction, with a diagram for each. You just have to learn it. Then cover the page and scribble down the main points from memory. Then try again, and again...

# Commercial Use of Hormones

*Plant Hormones*

Plant hormones have a lot of uses in the <u>food growing business</u>.

## 1) Controlling the Ripening of Fruit

1) The <u>ripening</u> of fruits can be controlled either while they are <u>still on the plant</u>, or during <u>transport</u> to the shops.

2) This allows the fruit to be picked while it's still <u>unripe</u> (and therefore firmer and <u>less easily damaged</u>).

3) It can then be sprayed with <u>ripening hormone</u> and it will ripen <u>on the way</u> to the supermarket to be perfect just as it reaches the shelves.

## 2) Growing from Cuttings with Rooting Compound

1) A <u>cutting</u> is part of a plant that has been <u>cut off</u>, like the end of a branch with a few leaves on it.

2) Normally, if you stick cuttings in the soil they <u>won't grow</u>, but if you add <u>rooting compound</u>, which is a plant <u>growth hormone</u>, they will produce roots rapidly and start growing as <u>new plants</u>.

3) This enables growers to produce lots of <u>clones</u> (exact copies) of a really good plant <u>very quickly</u>.

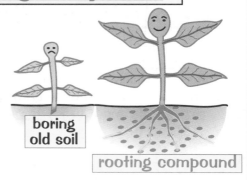

boring old soil

rooting compound

## 3) Killing Weeds

1) Most weeds growing in fields of crops or in a lawn are <u>broad-leaved</u>, in contrast to grass which has very <u>narrow leaves</u>.

2) <u>Selective weedkillers</u> have been developed from <u>plant growth hormones</u> which only affect the broad-leaved plants.

3) They totally <u>disrupt</u> their normal <u>growth patterns</u>, which soon <u>kills</u> them, whilst leaving the grass untouched.

Unhappy weeds

## 4) Producing Seedless Fruit

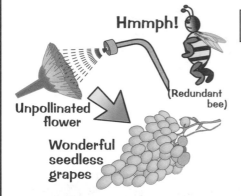

Hmmph!

(Redundant bee)

Unpollinated flower

Wonderful seedless grapes

1) Fruits normally only grow on plants which have been <u>pollinated by insects</u>, with the inevitable <u>seeds</u> in the middle of the fruit. If the plant <u>doesn't</u> get pollinated, the fruits and seeds <u>don't grow</u>.

2) However, if <u>growth hormones</u> are applied to <u>unpollinated flowers</u> the <u>fruits will grow</u> but the <u>seeds won't</u>.

3) This is great. Seedless satsumas and seedless grapes are just <u>so much nicer</u> than the 'natural' ones full of pips.

## Remember, serious learning always bears fruit...

Another blissfully easy page. Just make sure you learn enough about each bit to answer a 3 mark Exam question on it (that means being able to make 3 valid points). As usual the sections are split into numbered points to help you remember them. They've all got three points to learn. <u>So learn them</u>. Then <u>cover the page</u> and <u>scribble down</u> the 3 points for each. And tell me this: — if you can't do it now, what makes you think it'll all suddenly *"come back to you"* in the Exam?

# Energy and Biomass

Energy and biomass — they really aren't that hard.

## Biomass Pyramids describe food chains

1) This pyramid of biomass shows the <u>food chain</u> of a mini meadow ecosystem. The dandelions are the starting point or <u>provider</u>: they get eaten by the rabbits which, in turn, are eaten by the fox and so on.

2) <u>Biomass</u> is just how much all the creatures at each level would "<u>weigh</u>" if you <u>put them all together</u>.

3) The <u>dandelions</u> would have a <u>big biomass</u> and the <u>hundreds of fleas</u> would have <u>a very small biomass</u>. Biomass pyramids are <u>always a pyramid shape</u>:

Fleas
Fox
Rabbits
Dandelions

Each time you go up one level (one <u>trophic level</u> if you fancy showing off) the mass of organisms goes down. It takes a lot of food from the level below to keep any one animal alive.

## All that Energy just Disappears Somehow...

1) Energy from the <u>Sun</u> is the <u>source of energy</u> for <u>all life on Earth</u>.

2) <u>Plants</u> convert <u>a small %</u> of the light energy that falls on them <u>into glucose</u>. The <u>rabbit</u> then <u>eats</u> the <u>plant</u>. It <u>uses up</u> some of the energy it gets from the plant — some of the rest is <u>stored</u> in its body. Then the <u>fox eats</u> the <u>rabbit</u> and gets some of the energy stored in the rabbit's body.

At each stage of the food chain material and energy are lost.

This explains why you get <u>biomass pyramids</u>. Most of the biomass is lost and so does <u>not</u> become biomass in the <u>next level up</u>.

HEAT LOSS

MATERIALS LOST IN ANIMAL'S WASTE

3) The <u>energy lost</u> at each stage is used for <u>staying alive</u>, ie. in <u>respiration</u>, which powers <u>all life processes</u>, including <u>movement</u>.

4) Most of this energy is eventually <u>lost to the surroundings</u> as <u>heat</u>. This is especially true for <u>mammals and birds</u> whose bodies must be kept at a <u>constant temperature</u> — normally higher than their surroundings.

5) <u>Material and energy</u> is also lost from the food chain in the <u>droppings</u> — they burn when dried, proving they still have chemical energy in them.

*Try it next time you're camping — you'll find you enjoy your midnight sausages that much more when cooked over a blazing mound of dried sheep poo.*

## Pyramids of Biomass — the eighth wonder of the world...

Biomass pyramids are <u>hideously easy</u>. It's kiddies' coloured building block stuff. The bit about energy in the food chain needs a tiny bit more thought. A <u>mini-essay</u> is your best bet to learn it.

*Action of Microorganisms*

# Decomposition and Carbon Cycle

1) <u>Living things</u> are made of <u>materials</u> they take from the world around them.
2) When they <u>decompose</u>, ashes are returned to ashes, and dust to dust, as it were.
3) In other words <u>the elements they contain</u> are returned to the <u>soil</u> where they came from <u>originally</u>.
4) These elements are then <u>used by plants</u> to grow, and the whole cycle <u>repeats</u> over and over again.

## Decomposition *is carried out by Bacteria* **and** *Fungi*

1) All <u>plant matter</u> and <u>dead animals</u> are broken down (digested) by <u>microbes</u>.
2) This happens everywhere in <u>nature</u>, and also in <u>compost heaps</u> and <u>sewage works</u>.
3) All the important <u>elements</u> are thus <u>recycled</u>:
   <u>Carbon</u>, <u>Hydrogen</u>, <u>Oxygen</u> and <u>Nitrogen</u>.
4) The <u>ideal conditions</u> for creating <u>compost</u> are:
   a) <u>WARMTH</u>
   b) <u>MOISTURE</u>
   c) <u>GOOD OXYGEN (AIR) SUPPLY</u>
   d) <u>MICROORGANISMS</u> (i.e. <u>bacteria</u> and <u>fungi</u>)
   e) <u>ORGANIC MATTER</u> cut into <u>small pieces</u>.
      Make sure you <u>learn them</u> — all five.

Extra microbes added (compost maker)

Warmth generated by decomposition helps it all along

Finely shredded waste is best

Mesh sides to let air in

There's a bloke I know, and everyone calls him "the party mushroom". I'm not sure why really — they just say he's a fun guy to be with...

## The *Carbon Cycle* Shows how *Carbon* *is* *Recycled*

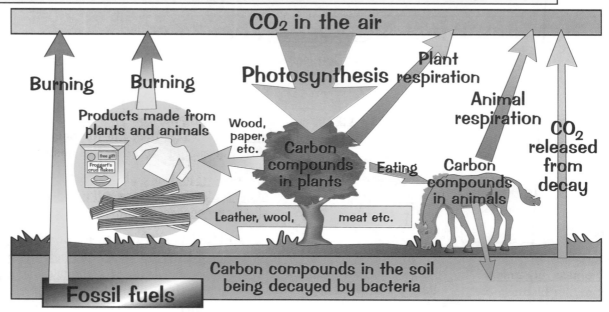

$CO_2$ in the air

Burning    Burning    Photosynthesis    Plant respiration

Animal respiration

$CO_2$ released from decay

Products made from plants and animals

Wood, paper, etc.

Carbon compounds in plants

Eating

Carbon compounds in animals

free gift / Froggatt's crud flakes

Leather, wool,    meat etc.

Fossil fuels

Carbon compounds in the soil being decayed by bacteria

This diagram isn't half as bad as it looks. <u>Learn</u> these important points:
1) There's only <u>one arrow</u> going <u>down</u>. The whole thing is "powered" by <u>photosynthesis</u>.
2) Both plant and animal <u>respiration</u> puts $CO_2$ <u>back into the atmosphere</u>.
3) <u>Plants</u> convert the carbon in $CO_2$ <u>from the air</u> into <u>fats</u>, <u>carbohydrates</u> and <u>proteins</u>.
4) These can then go <u>three ways</u>: <u>be eaten</u>, <u>be decayed</u> by microorganisms or be turned into <u>useful products</u> by man.
5) <u>Microorganisms</u> release $CO_2$ during the <u>decaying process</u>.
6) Ultimately these plant and animal products either <u>decay</u> or are <u>burned</u> and <u>$CO_2$ is released</u>.

## On Ilkley Moor baht 'at, On Ilkley Moor baht 'at...

Learn the five ideal conditions for compost making. They like asking about that.
Sketch out your <u>own simplified version</u> of the carbon cycle, making sure it contains all the labels.
Practise <u>scribbling</u> it out <u>from memory</u>. And <u>keep trying till you can</u>.

# Deforestation

Action of Microorganisms

## Deforestation increases CO₂ and the Greenhouse Effect

We have already pretty well deforested <u>our country</u>. Now many <u>under-developed</u> tropical countries are doing the same for fuel, urban development and farming.

Deforestation increases $CO_2$ in the atmosphere in two ways:

1) The trees unsuitable for timber are <u>burned</u>, releasing $CO_2$ directly into the atmosphere. Microbes also release $CO_2$ by <u>decaying</u> the felled trees that remain. This is resulting in an increase in atmospheric $CO_2$ levels.

2) Because living trees use $CO_2$ for <u>photosynthesis</u>, removing these trees means <u>less</u> $CO_2$ is removed from the atmosphere.

## Modern Industrial Life is Increasing the Greenhouse Effect

1) The level of <u>CO₂</u> in the atmosphere used to be nicely <u>balanced</u> between the $CO_2$ released by <u>respiration</u> (of animals and plants) and the $CO_2$ absorbed by <u>photosynthesis</u>.

2) However, mankind has been burning <u>massive amounts</u> of <u>fossil fuels</u> in the last two hundred years or so.

3) We have also been <u>cutting down trees</u> all over the world to make space for living and farming (<u>deforestation</u>).

4) The level of $CO_2$ in the atmosphere has <u>gone up</u> by about <u>20%</u>, and will <u>continue to rise</u> ever more steeply as long as we keep <u>burning fossil fuels</u> — just look at that graph — eek!

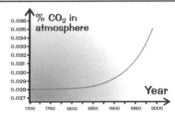

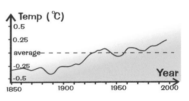

## Development has to be Sustainable

The Examiners' favourite phrase this year is '<u>sustainable development</u>'. They've gone <u>potty</u> about it.

> <u>SUSTAINABLE DEVELOPMENT</u> meets the needs of <u>today's</u> population <u>without</u> harming the ability of <u>future</u> generations to meet their own needs.

1) Farming and burning fossil fuels are necessary for our <u>standards of living</u> and there's <u>more demand</u> on them as the population gets <u>bigger</u>.

2) There's only so much <u>abuse</u> our little planet can take. Nowadays, developers <u>can't</u> just build huge power stations or shove stuff in landfills willy–nilly. They have to take greater care to <u>sustain</u> the <u>delicate balance</u> on Earth — the gases in the <u>atmosphere</u> and disposal of <u>waste</u> and the replanting of forestry are just three things they have to think about.

3) <u>Sustainable development</u> is environmentally friendly. Most development today <u>must</u> be able to continue into the <u>future</u> with as <u>little damage</u> as possible to the planet.

4) In the Exam, make sure you remember the details about the <u>environmental problems</u> development causes. If you get an essay-type question, stick 'em in and show off your '<u>scientific knowledge</u>'.

5) You'll have to weigh up the pros and cons too.
That's all an essay is — write about the <u>pros</u>, then the <u>cons</u>, then make a <u>conclusion</u>.

## Deforestation — where de train stops in de woods...

This is a really popular section for Examiners. Learn it well and impress them. Remember this — in your Science essays, you're marked on <u>what you know</u>, not what your conclusion is.

# The Nitrogen Cycle

Waste Material

Compared to the Carbon Cycle, the Nitrogen Cycle is really quite confusing.
To unravel it, you have to learn the diagram below and all 11 numbered points.

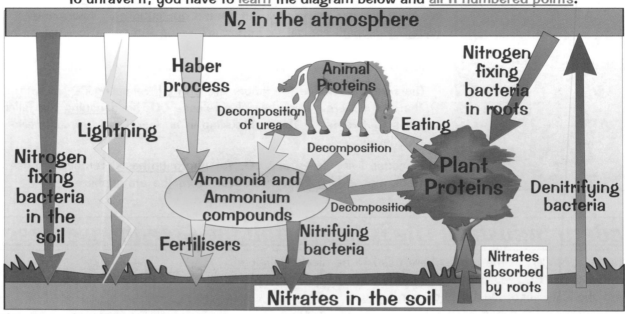

N₂ in the atmosphere

1) The atmosphere contains 78% nitrogen gas, $N_2$.
2) This is very unreactive and cannot be used directly by plants or animals.
3) Nitrogen is an important element in making protein and also DNA, so we really need it.
4) Nitrogen in the air has to be turned into nitrates, $NO_3^-$, or ammonium ions, $NH_4^+$, before plants can use it. Animals can only use proteins made by plants.
5) Nitrogen Fixation is the process of turning $N_2$ from the air into a more reactive form which plants can use (and no it isn't an obsession with breathing in and out).
6) There are THREE MAIN WAYS that it happens:   1) Lightning,      2) Nitrogen fixing bacteria in roots and soil,      3) The manufacture of artificial fertilisers by the Haber process.
7) There are four different types of bacteria involved in the nitrogen cycle:
    a) NITRIFYING BACTERIA — these turn ammonium compounds in decaying matter into useful nitrates.
    b) NITROGEN-FIXING BACTERIA — these turn useless atmospheric $N_2$ into useful nitrates.
    c) PUTREFYING BACTERIA (decomposers) — these decompose proteins and urea into ammonia or ammonium compounds.
    d) DE-NITRIFYING BACTERIA — these turn nitrates back into $N_2$ gas. This is of no benefit.
8) Some nitrogen-fixing bacteria live in the soil. Others live a mutualistic relationship with certain plants, called legumes, by living in nodules in their roots — the bacteria get food from the plant, and the plant gets nitrogen compounds from the bacteria — to make into proteins.
9) Any organic waste, ie. rotting plants or dead animals or animal poo, will contain useful nitrogen compounds (proteins), so they all make good fertiliser if they're put back into the soil.
10) Leguminous plants (legumes) such as clover are useful in crop rotation schemes, where the field is left for a year to just grow clover, and then it's all simply ploughed back into the soil. This adds a lot of nitrates to the soil when the plants decay.
11) Lightning adds nitrates to the soil by splitting up $N_2$ into nitrogen atoms which react with the oxygen in the air to form oxides of nitrogen. These then dissolve in rain, and fall to the ground where they combine with other things to form nitrates.

## By Gum, you young 'uns have some stuff to learn...

It's really "grisly grimsdike" is the Nitrogen Cycle, I think. But the fun guys at the Exam Boards want you to know all about it, so there you go. It's a mini-essay and a half, this one.

# Pesticides

Pesticides are artificial chemicals which are spread onto farm land in massive quantities every year. The damaging effects of this haven't always been spotted straight away.

## Pesticides Disturb Food Chains

1) Pesticides are sprayed onto most crops to kill the various insects that can damage the crops.

2) Unfortunately, they also kill lots of harmless insects such as bees and beetles.

3) This can cause a shortage of food for many insect-eating birds.

4) Pesticides tend to be poisonous and there's always the danger of the poison passing on to other animals (as well as humans).

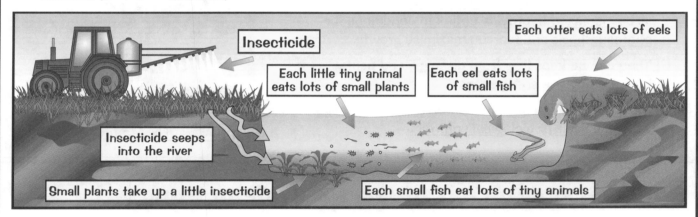

Insecticide

Each otter eats lots of eels

Each little tiny animal eats lots of small plants

Each eel eats lots of small fish

Insecticide seeps into the river

Small plants take up a little insecticide

Each small fish eat lots of tiny animals

This is well illustrated by the case of otters which were almost wiped out over much of crop-dominated Southern England by a pesticide called DDT in the early 1960s. The diagram shows the food chain which ends with the otter. DDT is not excreted so it accumulates along the food chain and the otter ends up with all the DDT collected by all the other animals.

## Pesticides do Some Useful Stuff

Pesticides must do something good as well — otherwise there'd be no point in using them. The farmer must protect his crop against infestation from insects and weeds so he doesn't lose it. Crops are worth a lot of money — it's far too costly to risk losing a whole yield.

1) Insecticides kill insects. Insects such as aphids, weevils and the dreaded Colorado beetle are responsible for an enormous amount of crop damage.

2) Herbicides kill weeds so they can't compete with the crops. Farmers don't want to plough the field and scatter the good seed on the expensively fertilized land for the benefit of weeds.

3) Fungicides kill fungi — especially mould. Farmers don't want their crops going mouldy before they've even been harvested.

## Revision — it can be a pest...

You could get asked in the Exam to write about the costs and benefits of intensive farming. That means you need to learn how pesticides can do both harm and good. Learn both sets of numbered points, and check you've learnt them. The diagram should make it all lovely and clear.

**Maximising Food Production**

# Managed Ecosystems

## Glass House Ecosystems

Glass houses have advantages for commercial food growing:

1) They trap the sun's warmth (the original Greenhouse Effect) making the plants grow faster than outside.

2) They enable us to grow plants out of season using heaters and artificial light.

3) The conditions can be completely controlled.

4) Carbon dioxide, light and temperature levels can all be increased to provide optimum conditions for photosynthesis and thereby maximise growth.

5) They can be kept free from diseases and pests by good hygiene and screens.

6) Pests are easy to see and can be controlled easily with chemicals or biological controls.

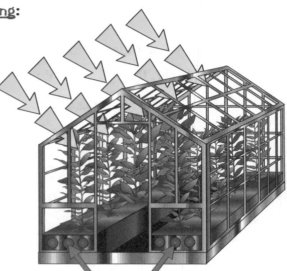

Under-soil heaters

## Biological Pest Control *Takes a While to Work*

To control pests in glass houses you can introduce predators to eat them, or sterile males to stop them breeding. Here are some ace examples:

1) The Aphidoletes midge lays larvae which eat aphids.
2) There's a special type of ladybird which attacks mealy bugs.
3) Encarsia is a tiny wasp which lays its eggs inside whitefly. The eggs hatch, and the wasp larvae eat the whitefly from the inside.
4) There's a tiny red mite called Phytoseiulus which attacks red spider mites.
5) Sterile males can be introduced to the swarm of pests so that reproduction can't happen — the fancy Biology name for this is autocide.

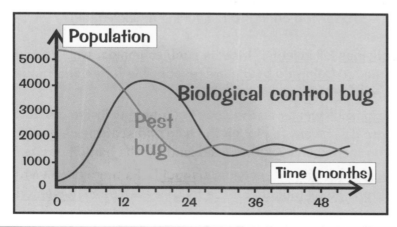

The graph shows the sort of time scales that can be involved in biological pest control and how the populations of pest and predator vary.

Notice it can take 18 months (that's 1½ years) for the pesky bug to be brought under control.
Both populations gradually settle down to a gently undulating pattern.

## Don't get bugged by Revision — just learn and enjoy...

Glass houses are a great example of a managed ecosystem. They're specifically mentioned in the syllabuses and may very well come up in your Exam. You could do many sillier things with 20 minutes than learn all these exciting facts. Learn the pros and cons of biological pest control, too.

# Biodiversity

Biodiversity... another <u>long Biology word</u> to learn.  How you must be smiling.

## Biodiversity — **How Many Types of Living Things**

<u>Learn</u> this definition of biodiversity.

> Biodiversity is the number of <u>different types</u> of <u>living things</u> in an <u>ecosystem</u>.

## Comparing **Biodiversity**

In the Exam they might give you data for how many different types of living thing there are in two different habitats. You just have to <u>compare the figures</u> — you don't have to do any <u>calculations</u>.

This one's <u>dead easy</u>.  You can see that there are fewer <u>types</u> of living thing in the desert than in the woodland.

**100m² Desert**
3 saguaro cactus
5 barrel cactus
4 tumbleweed
500 insects
2 lizards

**100m² Woodland**
9 oak trees          12 mice
30 bluebells        8 voles
900 moss plants   3 squirrels
40 000 insects     10 birds

They could also ask you to say what would happen if a habitat <u>changed</u>.  These questions are tougher.

**Example question:** What would happen to the biodiversity of woodlands in Yorkshire if half of them were cut down?

Answer: The biodiversity would <u>decrease</u>, for these reasons:

1) Amount of resources <u>decreases</u>.  Resources include light, water, food/nutrients from soil, space, etc
2) <u>Competition</u> for resources <u>increases</u>.  For example, if resources for small furry creatures were scarce, the habitat would be able to support fewer varieties of mouse.
3) Some organisms will be <u>wiped out</u> when the habitat is destroyed — which will <u>reduce</u> the <u>biodiversity</u>. For example, if all the thrush nests were cut down, there'd be no more thrushes.
4) If some organisms were wiped out, the <u>food chain</u> would be <u>disrupted</u>. This would affect the numbers of other organisms.

## Explaining **Biodiversity of Plants**

1) You might be given some data about the <u>number</u> of different plants in a habitat. Using your skill and judgement, you'd have to <u>explain</u> the <u>figures</u>.
2) You should write about the <u>physical factors</u> that affect how well different plants will grow — rainfall, temperature, soil quality etc. Eg: for a <u>desert habitat</u>, you'd write about <u>low rainfall</u>, high temperature and <u>poor soil quality</u>.
3) Make sure you mention how well different plants are <u>adapted</u> to the habitat (see Module 2 in the other book).  Eg: for a <u>desert habitat</u> which was mostly cactus and not much else, you'd say <u>cactuses</u> are <u>better adapted</u> than other plants to the hot, dry conditions.
4) You should also write about what <u>man</u> might be doing to the <u>habitat</u> — things like tree-felling, farming, use of pesticides etc.

## Biodiversity — seeing the wood for the trees...

Learn the <u>definition</u> of biodiversity <u>off by heart</u>.  Learn the different factors that affect biodiversity. Some of them are the <u>same factors</u> that affect <u>population size</u>.  If you learn them, you'll be able to apply them to <u>any habitat</u> they might give you in the Exam.  Take time to get your head round it.

Natural Ecosystems

# Conservation

Chop, chop, chop, oops they're homeless... and dead.

## Better Conservation means More Biodiversity

Conservation means managing ecosystems in order to protect habitats. A habitat with lots of lovely resources will support a larger biodiversity than a mangy old habitat with nothing to offer.

1) If ecosystems are managed in a controlled way,
   animal and plant populations will remain at a sustainable level.
2) If they're farmed or fished in an uncontrolled way, species
   will become endangered and (if nothing is done) extinct (at least in that locality).
3) When one species becomes locally extinct, it messes up the food chain for lots of other species.

## Example 1: The British Barn Owl is Dying Out

Barn Owls like open areas of rough grassland with hedgerows because this is where voles hang out. Apart from enjoying the company of voles, Barn Owls like to rip them to bits and swallow them. Barn Owls live and nest in barns (funny that) and old hollow trees.

Modern farming is destroying the Barn Owl habitat in three ways:

1) Replacing areas of rough grassland, hedgerows and trees with crop land.
2) Demolishing old farm buildings, or converting them into houses.
3) Overuse of pesticides which can poison voles and mice.

Also, some of the best remaining hunting ground is the rough grassland beside roads. As a result many Barn Owls are killed by passing traffic.

To save the Barn Owl we need to:
1) Replant hedgerows.
2) Allow areas of land to return to an undisturbed habitat to increase mice and vole numbers.
3) Provide nesting boxes in barns, and trees.

(These things are slowly being done as part of sustainable farming projects.)

## Example 2: Overfishing North Atlantic Cod

You'd think that cod were incredibly common — cod and chips isn't exactly a rarity. But, because of frenzied overfishing this tasty fish could be wiped out from the North Atlantic.

Don't panic yet, you crazy cod lovers — there's a four-pronged plan. Learn it well.

 1) Fishing quotas to control the numbers of fish killed.

 2) Ban on catching juvenile cod to make animal feed.

3) Fishing ban during the three month spawning period.

 4) Use of mesh nets that let the juvenile cod escape.

This recovery plan started in June 2001. If it works well, by June 2006 the North sea will produce 10 times more cod than were caught in 2000.

## Dodo in batter please...

Conservation questions are going to come up more and more in the exams so learn the examples. If they ask you for an example of habitat destruction give 'em the barn owl, if they ask for overfishing give 'em the cod story. You have to be able to relate it all to habitats and biodiversity.

# Revision Summary for Module Seven

*Jeepers creepers. Well, it's a stupidly long module, but it still all needs learning.*
*A quick way to do this is to make use of all the pictures — these are far easier to remember than just*
*lists and lists of facts. Once you know the pictures it's fairly simple to tag on any extra info. You'll*
*soon find that simply drawing the picture will help you recall the rest. So even if the question doesn't*
*ask for a picture it's still worth doing a quick sketch.*
*Same drill as usual with these questions — keep going till you know the lot.*
*Just remember to use pictures to help jog your memory.*

1) Sketch a typical plant cell with all its labels.
2) Sketch a typical plant and label the five important parts. Explain exactly what each bit does.
3) What does photosynthesis do? Write down the word equation for photosynthesis.
4) Sketch a leaf and show the four things needed for photosynthesis.
5) What is the definition of diffusion and why is it important for photosynthesis?
6) What are the three variable quantities which affect the rate of photosynthesis?
7) Sketch a graph for each one and explain the shape.
8) What seven things is the glucose produced by photosynthesis used for?
9) What are the two types of tubes in plants? Whereabouts are they found in plants?
10) List three features for both types of tube and sketch them both.
11) List the three main minerals needed for healthy plant growth and what they are needed for.
12) What are the three deficiency symptoms?
13) What is unusual about active uptake? How do roots use it?
14) Describe how roots and leaves are specialised for the exchange of materials.
15) How are minerals absorbed by the roots?
16) Give the full strict definition of osmosis. What does it do to plant and animal cells in water?
17) What is turgor pressure? How does it come about and what use is it to plants?
18) What is transpiration? What causes it? What benefits does it bring?
19) How do leaves help to limit transpiration? What does this mean for plants in drier climates?
20) What are the four factors which affect the rate of transpiration?
21) Explain what stomata do and how they do it.
22) What are auxins? Where are they produced?
23) There are four ways that auxins affect roots and shoots. Give full details for all four.
24) List the four commercial uses for plant hormones. Why are ripening hormones useful?
25) Where does the energy in a food chain originate?
26) How much energy and biomass pass from one trophic level to the next?
27) Where does the rest go?
28) What is the Carbon Cycle all to do with? Copy and fill in as much of it from memory as you can.
29) What effect does deforestation have on the atmosphere?
30) What is sustainable development? Why is it desirable?
31) What is the Nitrogen Cycle all about? Draw as much of it from memory as you can.
32) What do the four types of bacteria in the Nitrogen Cycle actually do?
33) What is the great bonus of modern farming methods? What are the drawbacks?
34) How do pesticides damage food chains? Give full details.
35) Why are chemical pesticides used?
36) Explain how greenhouse management maximises commercial food production.
37) Give two examples of biological pest control.
38) Give the definition of biodiversity.
39) Give three factors that affect biodiversity.
40) Explain how conservation can improve biodiversity.
41) Where do Barn Owls live and why?
42) What are the three ways that modern farming is affecting the owl's habitat?

**The Lungs**

# Lungs and Breathing

## The *Thorax*

Learn this diagram really well:

1) The <u>thorax</u> is the top part of your 'body' which is protected by the <u>ribcage</u>.

2) The <u>lungs</u> are like <u>big pink sponges</u>.

3) The <u>trachea</u> is made of strong cartilage rings to avoid collapsing. It splits into two tubes called "<u>bronchi</u>" (each one is a "<u>bronchus</u>"), one going to each lung.

4) The bronchi split into progressively smaller tubes called <u>bronchioles</u>.

5) The bronchioles finally end at small bags called <u>alveoli</u> where the gas exchange takes place.

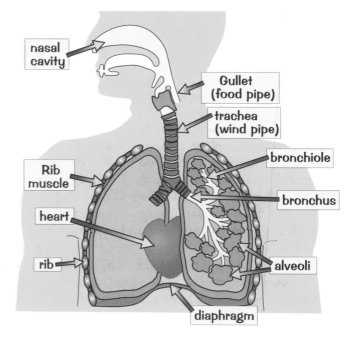

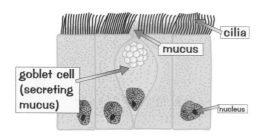

The membrane lining the <u>respiratory tract</u> (nasal passage, trachea and lungs) is lined with <u>mucus</u> and <u>cilia</u> (tiny little hairs) which catch <u>dust</u> and <u>bacteria</u> before they reach the lungs.

## Ventilation

Moving air <u>INTO</u> and <u>OUT OF</u> the lungs is called <u>VENTILATION</u>.

### Breathing In...

1) <u>Rib muscles</u> and <u>diaphragm</u> **CONTRACT**.
2) <u>Thorax volume</u> **INCREASES**.
3) Air is <u>DRAWN IN</u> due to decreased pressure.

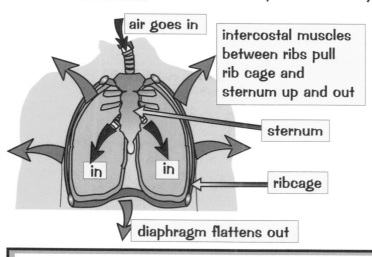

### ...and Breathing Out

1) <u>Rib muscles</u> and <u>diaphragm</u> **RELAX**.
2) <u>Thorax volume</u> **DECREASES**.
3) Air is <u>FORCED OUT</u> due to increased pressure.

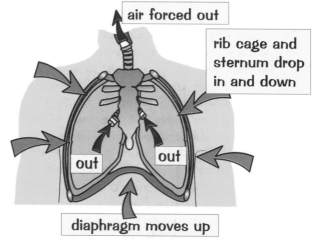

## Stop huffing and puffing and just LEARN IT...

No dreary lists of facts here, just three splendid diagrams and some breathing exercises. The only way to be sure you really know a diagram is to sketch it and label it, <u>all from memory</u>.

# Alveoli

*The Lungs*

Ah, the alveoli, where would we be without them? <u>Dead</u>, is the answer. So they're pretty important things. There's a <u>phenomenal number</u> of the little things in your lungs and it's here where the <u>oxygen</u> actually gets into the blood.

## Alveoli

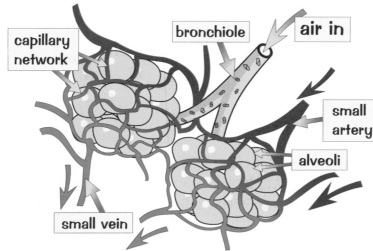

The <u>alveoli</u> are an ideal <u>exchange surface</u>. They have:

1) An <u>enormous surface area</u> (about 70m² in total).
2) A <u>moist lining</u> for dissolving gases.
3) Very <u>thin walls</u>.
4) A <u>copious blood supply</u>.

1) The job of the lungs is to <u>transfer oxygen to the blood</u> and to <u>remove waste carbon dioxide</u> from it.

2) To do this, <u>the lungs contain millions of alveoli</u> where <u>gas exchange</u> takes place.

## Gas Exchange at the Cells

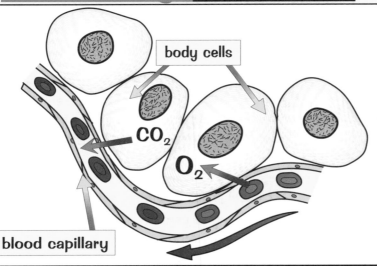

1) When the blood reaches the <u>cells</u>, <u>oxygen is released</u> from the red blood cells and <u>diffuses into the body cells</u>.

2) At the same time, <u>carbon dioxide diffuses into the blood</u> (plasma) to be carried back to the lungs.

## This is a very easy page to learn...

Notice that the numbered points repeat information that the diagrams already show very clearly. The big idea is that you should <u>understand and remember</u> what goes on and why it all works so well. A clear visual image in your head of these diagrams makes it a lot easier.
<u>Learn</u> the diagrams, words and all, until you can sketch them out <u>entirely from memory</u>.

# Smoking

*The Lungs*

Smoking is <u>no good</u> to <u>anyone</u> — except the cigarette companies.

## Cigarette Smoke *Wrecks the Lungs*

1) It <u>coats</u> the <u>inside of your lungs</u> with tar so they become <u>hideously inefficient</u>.

2) It covers the <u>cilia</u> in <u>tar</u> preventing them from getting bacteria out of your lungs.

3) The tar contains <u>carcinogens</u> which can cause lung cells to mutate to form <u>lung cancer</u>. A few years back, people didn't know this for sure but — out of every <u>ten</u> lung cancer patients, <u>nine</u> of them smoke. That's a pretty obvious connection.

4) Cigarette smoke can cause <u>emphysema</u>. This is a disease in which the <u>alveoli</u> lose their <u>stretchiness</u> and start to <u>break down</u>. This means the lungs can't <u>expand and contract properly</u>, and breathing becomes extremely <u>difficult</u>.

5) As the alveoli break down, the lungs are able to transfer <u>less and less oxygen</u> into the blood. Emphysema patients feel <u>out of breath</u>.

6) Cigarette smoke also causes <u>bronchitis</u>. Bronchitis is an inflammation of the bronchi and bronchioles. It causes the bronchioles to become clogged up with <u>thick mucus</u>, making <u>breathing difficult</u>.

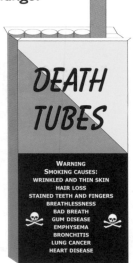

DEATH TUBES

WARNING
SMOKING CAUSES:
WRINKLED AND THIN SKIN
HAIR LOSS
STAINED TEETH AND FINGERS
BREATHLESSNESS
BAD BREATH
GUM DISEASE
EMPHYSEMA
BRONCHITIS
LUNG CANCER
HEART DISEASE

Cigarette smoke also causes diseases of the <u>heart</u> and <u>blood vessels</u>, leading to heart attacks and strokes. Smoking while <u>pregnant</u> deprives the foetus of <u>oxygen</u>, leading to a <u>small baby</u> at birth.

## *Giving Up* **is Hard — People Often** *Need Help*

Giving up cigarettes is <u>extremely hard</u>. A smoker's body gets <u>dependent</u> on nicotine. When a smoker stops taking nicotine, they get nasty withdrawal symptoms. They feel stressed and ratty. It is <u>possible</u> to give up, but it takes a lot of <u>determination</u>.

The most popular method of quitting is <u>cold turkey</u>. This is giving up without the use of anything — just deciding to stop and then stopping. Cold turkey requires <u>a lot of will power</u>.

There are other methods available to smokers who wish to give up. These include:

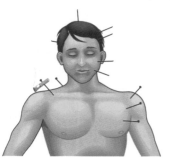

1) <u>Nicotine Replacement Therapy</u> — This method involves a slow let down from the dependency on nicotine. The smoker still takes nicotine into his body in the form of <u>nasal sprays</u>, <u>inhalers</u>, <u>patches</u> or <u>nicotine chewing gum</u>.

2) <u>Acupuncture</u> — Small <u>needles</u> are inserted into key pressure points on the body. There is no clinical proof this method works.

3) <u>Hypnotherapy</u> — "When I click my fingers you will no longer want to smoke". Again this is an unproven method.

Sounds like a lot of hassle to me, much better just <u>not smoking</u> in the first place.

## Smoking — *just learn the facts...*

You need to know about <u>lung cancer</u> and <u>emphysema</u>. Not only can they turn up in your exam but hopefully it'll make you think twice about starting to smoke. I'd recommend a <u>mini essay</u> for that part of the page. The methods of <u>stopping smoking</u> need learning too — cover and scribble.

# The Circulatory System

*The Circulation*

The circulatory system's main function is to get food and oxygen to every cell in the body.
The diagram shows the basic layout, but make sure you learn the five important points too.

## The DOUBLE Circulatory System, *actually*

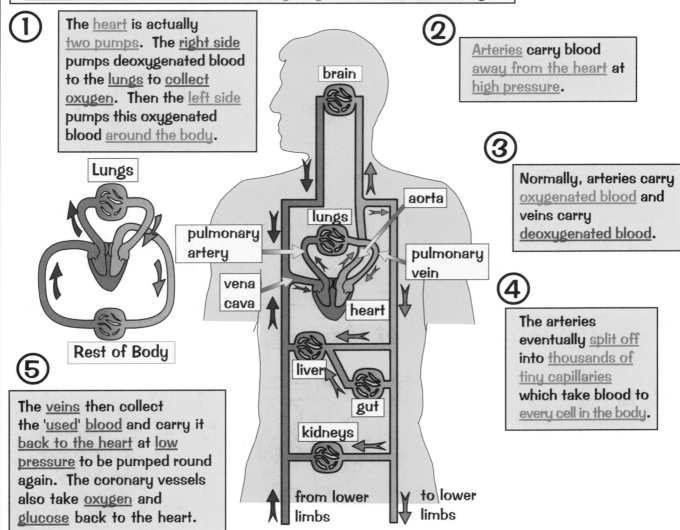

① The heart is actually two pumps. The right side pumps deoxygenated blood to the lungs to collect oxygen. Then the left side pumps this oxygenated blood around the body.

② Arteries carry blood away from the heart at high pressure.

③ Normally, arteries carry oxygenated blood and veins carry deoxygenated blood.

④ The arteries eventually split off into thousands of tiny capillaries which take blood to every cell in the body.

⑤ The veins then collect the 'used' blood and carry it back to the heart at low pressure to be pumped round again. The coronary vessels also take oxygen and glucose back to the heart.

## Red blood cells are Designed to Carry Oxygen

1) Their job is to carry oxygen to the rest of the blood.
2) Blood cells have a flying doughnut shape to give the maximum surface area for absorbing oxygen. The shape also gives them a smooth journey through the capillaries.
3) They contain haemoglobin, which is very red, and which contains a lot of iron. Haemoglobin holds and carries oxygen.
4) They don't have a nucleus. This creates more room for haemoglobin. They don't need a nucleus anyway.

## Let's see what you know then...

At least this stuff on the circulatory system is fairly interesting. Mind you, there are still plenty of picky little details you need to be clear about. And yes, you've guessed it, there's one sure-fire way to check just how clear you are — read it, learn it, then cover the page and reproduce it.
Having to sketch the diagram out again from memory is the only way to really learn it.

# Pumping Cycle

*The Circulation*

The heart is made almost entirely of <u>muscle</u>. And it's a <u>double pump</u>.
Visualise this diagram with its <u>bigger side</u> full of <u>red, oxygenated blood</u>, and its
<u>smaller side</u> full of <u>blue, deoxygenated blood</u>, and learn that the <u>left side</u> is <u>bigger</u>.

## Learn **This** Diagram **of the** Heart **with All its** Labels

### Right Side                    ### Left Side

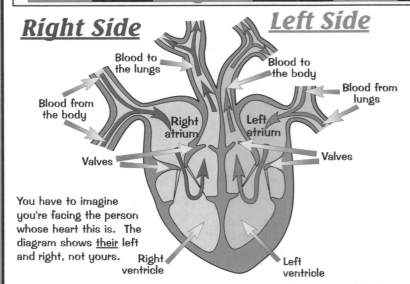

You have to imagine
you're facing the person
whose heart this is. The
diagram shows <u>their</u> left
and right, not yours.

1) The <u>right side</u> of the heart receives <u>deoxygenated blood</u> from the body and pumps it only to the <u>lungs</u>, so it has <u>thinner walls</u> than the left side.

2) The <u>left side</u> receives <u>oxygenated blood</u> from the lungs and pumps it out round the <u>whole body</u>, so it has <u>thicker, more muscular walls</u>.

3) The <u>ventricles</u> are <u>much bigger</u> than the <u>atria</u> because they push blood <u>round the body</u>.

4) The <u>valves</u> are for <u>preventing backflow</u> of blood.

## Learn the *Three Stages* of The *Pumping Cycle*

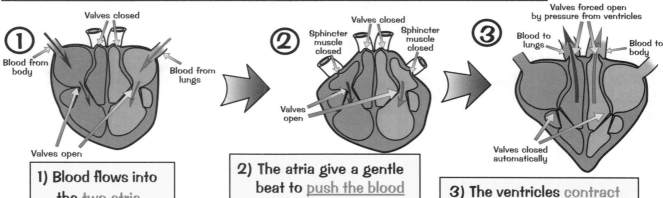

1) Blood flows into the <u>two atria</u>.

2) The atria give a gentle beat to <u>push the blood into the ventricles</u>.

3) The ventricles <u>contract</u> forcing <u>blood</u> out to the <u>lungs and body</u>.

The <u>ventricles</u> are much more <u>powerful</u>, and when they beat the <u>valves</u> between the atria and ventricles pop shut automatically <u>to prevent backflow</u> into the atria. Sphincters wouldn't be strong enough.

4) The blood flows <u>down the arteries</u>, the <u>atria fill again</u> and the whole cycle starts over.

As soon as the ventricles relax, <u>valves shut</u> to prevent backflow of blood (back into the ventricles) as it is now under <u>a fair bit of pressure</u> in the arteries. It's the <u>pressure</u> in the <u>arteries</u> which causes your <u>pulse</u>.

## OK, let's get to the heart of the matter...

You need to know the details of the heart and each step of the pumping cycle.
There's only one way to be sure you know it all and that's to learn the diagrams until you can
sketch them out, with all the labels, <u>from memory</u>. Also <u>learn</u> all the points for each section.

# Arteries and Veins

There are <u>three</u> different types of <u>blood vessel</u> and you need to know about all three.

## Arteries *Carry Blood Under* Pressure

1) <u>Arteries</u> carry oxygenated blood <u>away from the heart</u>.
2) It comes out of the heart at <u>high pressure</u>, so the artery walls have to be <u>strong and elastic</u>.
3) Note how <u>thick</u> the walls are compared to the size of the hole down the middle (the "lumen" — silly name!).

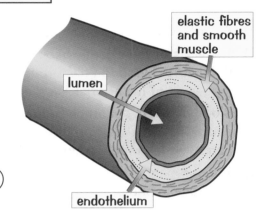

elastic fibres and smooth muscle

lumen

endothelium

## Capillaries *are Really* Small

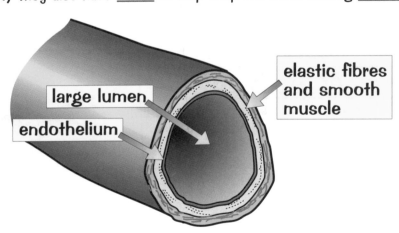

thin endothelium only one cell thick

very small lumen

nucleus of cell

1) Capillaries <u>deliver food and oxygen</u> direct to the body tissues and <u>take waste products away</u>.
2) Their walls are usually <u>only one cell thick</u> to make it easy for stuff <u>to pass in and out of them</u>.
3) They are <u>too small</u> to see.

## Veins *Take Blood* Back *to The Heart*

1) <u>Veins</u> carry <u>deoxygenated blood</u> back to the heart.
2) The blood is at <u>lower pressure</u> in the veins so <u>the walls do not need to be so thick</u>.
3) They have a <u>bigger lumen</u> than arteries <u>to help blood flow</u>.
4) They also have <u>valves</u> to help keep the blood flowing <u>in the right direction</u>.

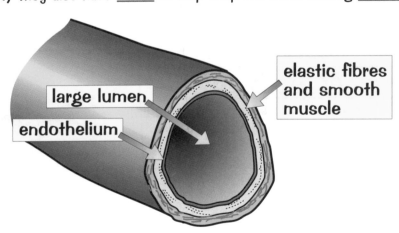

large lumen

endothelium

elastic fibres and smooth muscle

## Don't struggle in vein...

Let's face it these are mighty easy diagrams to learn. Just make sure you learn the numbered points as well. I reckon it can't take more than two or three attempts before you can scribble out the whole of this page, diagrams and all, <u>entirely from memory</u>. <u>Concentrate on learning the bits you forgot each time</u>, of course. Try it and see how right I am!

# Heart Disease and Lifestyle

*The Circulation*

Horrible stuff, heart disease.

## Heart Disease *and* Arteriosclerosis

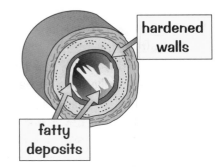

1) <u>Fat deposits</u> form on the inside of the <u>arteries</u>. This makes the arteries thinner, which obstructs the flow of blood.

2) The walls of the arteries become <u>harder</u>. This makes it more difficult for blood to flow through. The <u>narrowing</u> and <u>hardening</u> of the arteries is called <u>arteriosclerosis</u>.

3) Blood platelets get stuck to the fatty deposits. This can cause the blood flowing through to <u>clot</u>. If the arteries have narrowed too much, a blood clot can <u>block</u> them completely.

4) The <u>coronary arteries</u> supply the <u>heart muscle</u> with blood rich in oxygen and glucose. A blockage in one of the <u>coronary arteries</u> prevents oxygen and glucose from reaching part of the heart. That part of the heart then stops working. This is called <u>coronary heart disease</u>.

5) A complete blockage in one of the bigger coronary arteries causes a <u>heart attack</u>.

6) In a heart attack, the blood supply to a big chunk of the heart muscles is blocked and the <u>heart stops beating</u> altogether. If blood supply is not restored, the heart muscle cells will be <u>damaged beyond repair</u>. Basically, they die. If your heart muscle dies, then you die.

## Lifestyle *Affects the* Circulatory System

1) Eating a lot of <u>fat</u> and <u>cholesterol</u> is linked with heart disease (those fat deposits on the walls of the arteries have to come from somewhere). <u>Saturated fats</u> (eg lard, bacon fat) are <u>worse</u> for you than <u>unsaturated fats</u> (eg sunflower oil, olive oil).

2) Seriously <u>overweight</u> (obese) people are at higher risk of heart disease.

3) <u>Exercise</u> is the <u>best way</u> to a healthy heart. It makes the whole circulatory system more efficient at pumping blood around the body.

4) Exercise also <u>reduces</u> heart disease <u>risk factors</u> such as <u>obesity</u> and <u>high blood pressure</u>. It also improves muscle tone and makes you feel good.

5) <u>Smoking</u> increases the risk of heart disease.

## Fitness *is Good* — Steroid Abuse *is Bad*

Steroids are <u>hormones</u>. Artificial <u>anabolic steroids</u> can be used to <u>increase muscle growth</u>. Their legitimate use is to treat muscle-wasting conditions. They are <u>abused</u> by some athletes and others to <u>increase muscle mass</u> and improve <u>performance</u>. Unfortunately, steroid abuse has some rather <u>nasty side effects</u>:

1) <u>Liver cancer</u> and <u>jaundice</u>.
2) <u>High blood pressure</u> and <u>heart disease</u>.
3) Wild <u>mood swings</u> and <u>paranoia</u>.
4) In <u>men</u>, baldness, breast growth and shrunken testicles. (!!) Beard growth for <u>women</u>. (!!)

## A good heart these days is hard to find...

You are expected to know what arteriosclerosis is and how it affects the heart. Try a quick <u>mini-essay</u> about the <u>mechanics</u> of heart disease, and another on the <u>causes</u> of heart disease. The steroid stuff could pop up in a question about <u>exercise and fitness</u>, or in one about <u>hormones</u>.

# Insulin and Diabetes

The Circulation

Insulin is a hormone which controls how much sugar there is in your blood.  LEARN how:

## Insulin Controls Blood Sugar Levels

1) Eating foods containing carbohydrate puts a lot of glucose into the blood from the gut.
2) Normal metabolism of cells removes glucose from the blood.
3) Vigorous exercise removes much more glucose from the blood.
4) Obviously, to keep the level of blood glucose controlled there has to be a way
   to add or remove glucose from the blood.  This is achieved by a hormone
   called insulin which is released by the pancreas.

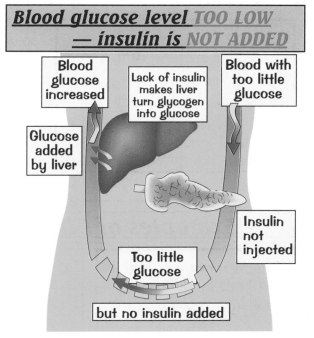

**Blood glucose level TOO HIGH — insulin is ADDED**

Blood glucose reduced

Insulin makes liver turn glucose into glycogen

Blood with too much glucose

Glucose removed by liver

Insulin

Too much glucose

Insulin injected by pancreas

but insulin as well

**Blood glucose level TOO LOW — insulin is NOT ADDED**

Blood glucose increased

Lack of insulin makes liver turn glycogen into glucose

Blood with too little glucose

Glucose added by liver

Too little glucose

Insulin not injected

but no insulin added

Remember, the addition of insulin reduces the blood sugar level.

## Diabetes — the Pancreas Stops Making Enough Insulin

1) Diabetes is a disease in which the pancreas doesn't produce enough insulin.
2) The result is that a person's blood sugar can rise to a level that can kill them.
3) The problem can be controlled in two ways:

A) Eating a sensible diet and taking regular exercise.

B) Injecting insulin daily.  This will make the liver remove the glucose from the blood
   as soon as it enters it from the gut, when the (carbohydrate-rich) food is being digested.
   This stops the level of glucose in the blood from getting too high and is
   a very effective treatment.

We use bacteria to produce human insulin for diabetes sufferers.  The human insulin
gene is spliced into the bacterium's DNA .  The big benefit of this is that real human
insulin is used.  Before gene splicing technology, diabetics had to use pig insulin.

## Learn all this stuff about blood sugar and diabetes...

This stuff on blood sugar and insulin can seem a bit confusing at first, but if you concentrate on
learning those two diagrams, it'll start to get a lot easier.  Don't forget that only carbohydrate
foods put the blood sugar levels up.  Learn it all, then cover the page and scribble it down.

Respiration,
Energy & Exercise

# Diffusion

## Diffusion — the Tendency of Things to Spread Out

"Diffusion" is the gradual net movement of particles from places where there are lots of them to places where there are fewer of them.  See P.3 for diffusion in plants.
Here's the definition again — make sure you learn it.

> ### DIFFUSION is the NET MOVEMENT OF PARTICLES from an area of HIGH CONCENTRATION to an area of LOW CONCENTRATION

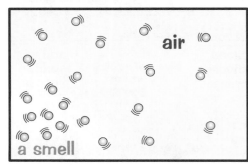

air

a smell

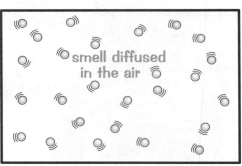

smell diffused
in the air

## Three Examples of Diffusion in the Body

1) Oxygen enters the blood in the lungs by diffusion...

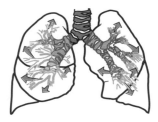

... and then diffuses out of the blood and into body tissues.

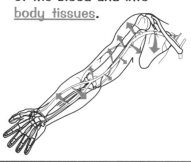

2) Carbon dioxide enters the blood in the body tissues...

...and then leaves the blood in the lungs.

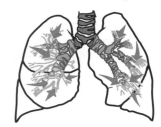

3) Food diffuses across the wall of the small intestine and into the blood.

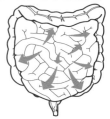

It then diffuses out of the blood and into various body tissues.

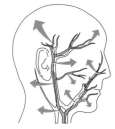

When food or gases are moving in and out of the blood — that's diffusion.  Remember that.

## So, how much do you know about diffusion...

Diffusion is a word that crops up a lot in this module.  You'll be expected to mention diffusion if you get a question about gas transfer in breathing.  Make sure you know what it means.

# Respiration

Food wouldn't be half as good if we didn't get energy from it.
Respiration is the name of the process where the body makes energy from food and oxygen.

## Glucose Molecules Can Diffuse into the Blood

Glucose is the body's fuel. Cells need glucose to make energy. It travels to the cells in the same way as oxygen, in the bloodstream. The difference is that instead of coming from the lungs, glucose is picked up by the blood in the digestive system.

1) Glucose molecules are small enough to diffuse from the gut into the blood.

2) They then travel to where they're needed, and diffuse from a capillary into a cell.

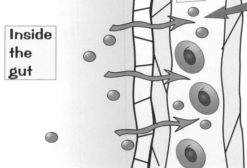

blood flows from gut to body cells

Inside the gut

The glucose molecules diffuse into the blood...

...and then out again somewhere else...

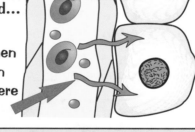

3) With oxygen and glucose present in the cell the respiration process can start.

4) The waste product of respiration, carbon dioxide, diffuses back into the blood to be taken to the lungs and exhaled.

## Respiration is NOT "breathing in and out"

1) Respiration is NOT breathing in and breathing out, as you might think.
2) Respiration actually goes on in every cell in your body.
3) Respiration is the process of converting glucose to energy.
4) It takes place in plants too. All living things "respire". They convert "food" into energy.

### RESPIRATION is the process of CONVERTING GLUCOSE TO ENERGY, which goes on in EVERY CELL

5) Energy released by respiration is used for four things:
   a) building larger molecules from smaller ones
   b) contracting muscles
   c) maintaining a steady body temperature
   d) powering active transport

## One big deep breath — then learn it...

You need to learn three things from this page: what respiration is, what two things it needs, and how those two things get to all the cells of the body. Usual method — read it, cover it up, scribble it down. Oh, and don't get respiration and breathing muddled up. You'll only kick yourself.

# Respiration

You know why things respire. "But,"I hear you ask, "how do they respire?" You're in for a treat now.

## Aerobic Respiration Needs Plenty of Oxygen

1) Aerobic respiration is what happens if there's plenty of oxygen available.

2) Aerobic just means "with oxygen" and it's the ideal way to convert glucose into energy.

You need to learn the word equation:

$$\text{Glucose + Oxygen} \rightarrow \text{Carbon Dioxide + Water + Energy}$$

4) During exercise, more oxygen is needed — so your heart rate and breathing increase to pump more oxygenated blood to your cells.

5) As oxygenated blood reaches the cells, the diffusion of oxygen into (and $CO_2$ out of) muscle cells increases.

## Anaerobic Respiration doesn't use Oxygen at all

1) Anaerobic respiration is what happens if your muscles are not supplied with enough oxygen. "Anaerobic" means "without oxygen".

2) This incomplete breakdown of glucose is NOT the best way to convert glucose into energy because it produces lactic acid. You need to learn the word equation:

$$\text{Glucose} \rightarrow \text{Energy + Lactic Acid}$$

3) Anaerobic respiration does not produce nearly as much energy as aerobic respiration — but it's useful in emergencies.

## Fitness and the Oxygen Debt

1) During vigorous exercise, your body can't supply enough oxygen to your muscles. They get fatigued and can stop contracting efficiently.

2) To get the energy they need, muscles start using anaerobic respiration instead. This incomplete breakdown of glucose produces a build up of lactic acid in the muscles, which gets painful — this is cramp. Ouch.

3) The advantage is that at least you can keep on using your muscles for a while longer.

4) After resorting to anaerobic respiration, when you stop you'll have an oxygen debt.

5) In other words you have to "repay" the oxygen which you didn't manage to get to your muscles in time, because your lungs, heart and blood couldn't keep up with the demand earlier on.

6) This means you have to keep breathing hard for a while after you stop to get oxygen into your muscles to oxidise the painful lactic acid into harmless $CO_2$ and water.

## Panting to reduce your debt — don't try it at the bank...

Learn the two word equations for aerobic and anaerobic respiration off by heart — and learn the numbered points, too. For the Oxygen Debt bit of the page, a mini-essay is your best bet. Remember, unlike normal debts, you don't have to pay interest on an oxygen debt. Enjoy.

# Inherited Diseases

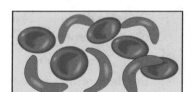

The diseases below are genetic diseases. People with these diseases are born with them. They are inherited from parents and are carried in the form of defective or altered genes.

## Cystic Fibrosis Affects the Lungs and Digestion

1) Cystic Fibrosis is a genetic disease which affects about 1 in 1600 people in the UK.

2) It's caused by a defective gene on one of the chromosomes which the person inherits from their parents. There's still no cure or fully effective treatment for this condition.

3) The result of the defective gene is that the body produces a lot of thick sticky mucus in the lungs, which has to be removed by massage.

4) Excess mucus also occurs in the pancreas, causing digestive problems.

5) Much more seriously though, the blockage of the air passages in the lungs causes a lot of chest infections.

6) Physiotherapy and antibiotics clear them up but slowly the sufferer becomes more and more ill.

## Sickle Cell Anaemia Affects the Blood

1) This disease causes the red blood cells to be shaped like sickles instead of the normal round shape.

2) They then get stuck in the capillaries. This deprives the body cells of oxygen.

3) It's an unpleasant, painful disease and sufferers die at an early age.

4) Yet even though sufferers die before they can reproduce, the occurrence of sickle cell anaemia doesn't always die out as you'd expect it to, especially not in Africa.

5) This is because carriers of the recessive allele which causes it ARE MORE IMMUNE TO MALARIA. Hence, being a carrier increases their chance of survival in some parts of the world, even though some of their offspring are going to die young from sickle cell anaemia.

6) The genetics are identical to Cystic Fibrosis because both diseases are caused by a recessive allele. Hence if BOTH parents are carriers each child has a 1 in 4 chance of having the disease.

## Cystic Fibrosis is Caused by a Recessive Gene (Allele)

The genetics behind cystic fibrosis and sickle cell anaemia are actually very straightforward. The gene which causes cystic fibrosis is a recessive gene, c, carried by about 1 person in 20. That means there's a 1 in 400 chance that two carriers will have children together. The usual genetic inheritance diagram illustrates what goes on:

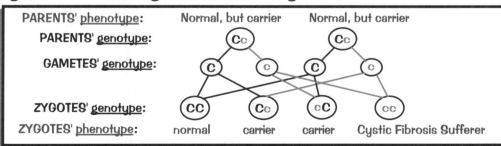

The diagram shows the 1 in 4 chance of a child having the disease, if both parents are carriers. This makes the overall probability 1 in 1600. This type of diagram applies to sickle cell anaemia as well.

## Learn the page then test yourself...

The symptoms should be relatively easy to learn. They're just lists of numbered points, after all. If it's been a while since you revised genes and inheritance, you might need to look at Module Two in the other book to remind yourself what recessive genes and phenotypes are.

*Inherited Diseases*

# Gene Therapy and Testing

Cystic fibrosis is the example on this page. They could ask you about other genetic diseases in the Exam, so remember that the same goes for them, too.

## Gene Therapy helps Cystic Fibrosis Symptoms

People with cystic fibrosis have a defective copy of a gene. The normal version of the gene makes a protein that keeps lung mucus thin and liquid. The defective gene makes lung mucus thick and sticky.

Gene therapy involves introducing the normal version of the gene into the cells of a sufferer's body. With the normal gene, the cells can make the missing protein.

In the gene therapy for cystic fibrosis, copies of the normal gene (packaged in a virus) are squirted right into the lungs with an inhaler. The cells of the lining of the lungs can start making the right form of the protein, and the lung mucus gets thinner and less sticky.

## Gene Therapy Doesn't Stop the Disease getting Passed On

1)  Genetic diseases like cystic fibrosis are passed on by a gene on one of the chromosomes in the egg or sperm cells in a carrier's or sufferer's body.

2)  Gene therapy does not rewrite the genetic code in the cells of the sufferer's body.

3)  Carriers and sufferers still have a copy of the faulty gene in every cell in their body.

## Genetic Testing Identifies Carriers

There are two ways to identify people who carry the gene for a genetic disease, eg. cystic fibrosis.

1)  Pedigree analysis involves looking back at the family tree and seeing which members of the family have been affected by the disease.
2)  Genetic testing involves looking at the actual genes.

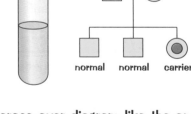

Genetic counselling is the next stop after genetic testing.

1)  People who are carrying the gene for cystic fibrosis, and who want to have children can go to a genetic counsellor for advice.
2)  The genetic counsellor explains the risk of any future children carrying the disease or suffering from the disease.
3)  The genetic counsellor needs to explain the genetic risk carefully. A cross-over diagram like the one on the previous page shows that two carriers have a 1 in 2 chance of having a child who carries the disease and a 1 in 4 chance of having a child who suffers from the disease. The couple might think that they'd have to have 4 children for the ratios to work out properly, which isn't quite true.

It's possible to test a foetus for some genetic diseases while it's still in the womb. If the foetus is carrying the gene for a genetic disease, or a chromosomal disorder like Down's Syndrome, the parents will have to decide whether to continue with the pregnancy or terminate it. This is a very difficult decision to make.

Some people feel that genetic diseases shouldn't be bred out of the population. They think it's equivalent to discrimination against people with genetic diseases.

*Higher*    *Higher*    *Higher*    *Higher*

## What's the risk of this being in the Exam, then...

Gene therapy sounds weird. It's not exactly a cure for inherited diseases — it just stops the symptoms flaring up. You've got to be able to say why it doesn't stop the disease being passed on to new generations. Genetic testing and counselling is another bit of Biology with issues.

# Revision Summary for Module Eight

*Phew, there's a lot of stuff to learn in Module Eight. And it's all that grisly "open heart surgery" type stuff too, with all those gory diagrams. Mind you, it's all fairly straightforward and factual — nothing difficult to understand, just lots of facts to learn. You know the big plan with these questions though. Keep practising till you can whizz them all off without a moment's hesitation on any of them. It's a nice trick if you can do it.*

1) Draw a diagram of the thorax, showing all the breathing equipment.
2) What is 'ventilation'?
3) Describe what happens during breathing in and breathing out. Be sure to give all the details.
4) Where are alveoli found? How big are they and what are they for? Give four features.
5) What two gases are exchanged in the lungs?
6) Describe the three main lung diseases that result from smoking.
7) List three methods people use to help them quit smoking.
8) Draw a diagram of the human circulatory system: heart, lungs, arteries, veins, etc.
9) Explain why it is a *double* circulatory system, and describe the pressure and oxygen content of the blood in each bit. What are the big words for saying if the blood has oxygen in or not?
10) Sketch a red blood cell and say what it does.
11) Draw a full diagram of the heart with all the labels. Explain how the two halves differ.
12) How do ventricles and atria compare, and why?
13) What are the valves in the heart for?
14) Describe briefly with diagrams the three stages of the pumping cycle for the heart.
15) Sketch an artery, a capillary, and a vein, with labels, and explain the features of all three.
16) What happens in arteriosclerosis?
17) What exactly happens in a heart attack?
18) Give two reasons why anabolic steroids might be taken. List the four drawbacks.
19) Explain, with diagrams, exactly what happens with insulin when the blood sugar is too high and when it is too low?
20) What is diabetes? Describe the two ways that it can be controlled.
21) What is the proper definition of diffusion?
22) Give three examples of diffusion in the body.
23) What is 'respiration'? Give a proper definition.
24) What is "aerobic respiration"? Give the word equation for it.
25) What is "anaerobic respiration"? Give the word equation for what happens in our bodies.
26) Why do your muscles hurt during vigorous exercise? What is the oxygen debt?
27) List the symptoms and treatment of cystic fibrosis. What causes this disease?
28) Draw a genetic diagram to show the probability of a child being a sufferer.
29) How does the overall probability of being a sufferer of cystic fibrosis work out to 1 in 1600?
30) Give the cause and symptoms of sickle cell anaemia. Why does it not die out?
31) How does gene therapy relieve symptoms of cystic fibrosis?
32) Why does gene therapy not prevent cystic fibrosis being passed on to the next generation?
33) Describe two ways in which carriers of genetic diseases can be identified.
34) What are the issues relating to the genetic testing of foetuses?

# Uses of Metals

*Metals*

Metals are a lot more interesting than most people ever realise.   (Classic chat-up line No. 71)

## Iron is made into _steel_ which is _cheap and strong_

Iron and steel:
    Advantages:    Cheap and strong.
    Disadvantages:  Heavy, and prone to rusting away.

Iron and steel are used for:
1) Construction such as bridges and buildings.
2) Cars and lorries and trains and boats and NOT PLANES and pushbikes and tanks and pianos...
3) Stainless steel doesn't rust and is used for pans and for fixtures on boats.

Steel may rust and it may not be exactly "space age" but it's strong and it's awful cheap, and it still has a lot of uses. They make cars out of it for one thing... but gone are the halcyon days when car bodies were hand-crafted from ash frames and lovingly honed to perfection. Now they just shovel them out of big presses by the million. Sigh. Mind you there's still the Morgan...

## Aluminium is _light_, strong _and_ _corrosion-resistant_

Strictly speaking you shouldn't say it's "light", you should say it has "low density". Whatever. All I know is, it's a lot easier to lift and move around than iron or steel.

Useful Properties:
1) Lightweight. (OK, "low density". Happy now?)
2) Can be bent and shaped (for making car body panels, etc.)
3) Strong and very rigid when required.
4) Doesn't corrode due to the protective layer of oxide which always quickly covers it.
5) It's also a good conductor of heat and electricity.

Drawbacks:  Not as strong as steel and a bit more expensive.

Common uses:
1) Ladders.
2) Aeroplanes.
3) Range Rover body panels (but not the rusty tailgate!).
4) Drink cans — better than tin-plated steel ones which can rust if damaged.
5) Greenhouses and window frames.
6) Big power cables used on pylons.

## Copper: _good conductor_, _easily bent_ and _doesn't corrode_

This is a winning combination which makes it ideal for:
1) Water pipes and gas pipes, because it can be bent to shape by hand without fracturing.
2) Electrical wiring because it can be easily bent round corners and it conducts really well.
3) Forms useful non-corroding alloys such as brass (for trumpets) and bronze (for statues).

Drawbacks:  Copper is quite expensive and is not strong.

## The Exciting Properties of Metals — learn and enjoy...

Well now, what have we here! Some chemistry which is useful in your everyday life! I reckon it's really pretty helpful if you know the difference between various different metals, although I guess it's only really important if you plan to build your own steam engine or rocket or something. If you don't, then you'll just have to learn it for the Exam and be done with it.

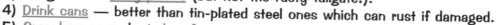

# Metal Ores

Unfortunately metal doesn't grow on trees. It has to be extracted.

## Rocks, Minerals and Ores

1) A <u>rock</u> is a mixture of <u>minerals</u>.
2) A <u>mineral</u> is any <u>solid element or compound</u> found naturally in the <u>Earth's crust</u>.
   Examples: Diamond (carbon), quartz (silicon dioxide), bauxite ($Al_2O_3$).
3) A <u>metal ore</u> is defined as a <u>mineral</u> or minerals which contain <u>enough metal</u> to make it <u>worthwhile</u> extracting the metal. There's a <u>limited amount</u> of minerals and ores — they're "<u>finite resources</u>".
4) The <u>more reactive</u> metals took <u>longer</u> to be discovered (eg. aluminium, sodium).
5) The <u>more reactive</u> metals are also <u>harder to extract</u> from their mineral ores.
6) The above <u>two facts</u> are obviously <u>related</u>. It's <u>obvious</u> when you think about it...

## Metals need to be extracted from their ore by reduction

Oxidation and reduction are all about the losing or gaining of electrons.

### OXIDATION
**Loss of Electrons**
<u>Oxidation</u> is the <u>addition of oxygen</u>.
Iron becoming iron oxide is oxidation.
The more technical and general definition of oxidation is "<u>the loss of electrons</u>".

### REDUCTION
**Gain of Electrons**
<u>Reduction</u> is the <u>loss of oxygen</u>.
Copper oxide is <u>reduced</u> to copper.
The more technical and general definition of reduction is "<u>the gain of electrons</u>".

Remember "OIL RIG" (Oxidation Is Loss, Reduction Is Gain)

## Metals are Extracted using Carbon or Electrolysis

1) <u>Extracting a metal</u> from its ore involves a <u>chemical reaction</u> to separate the metal out.
2) In many cases the metal is found as an <u>oxide</u>.
3) The <u>two</u> common ways of <u>extracting a metal</u> from its ore are:
   a) Chemical <u>reduction</u> using <u>carbon</u> or <u>carbon monoxide</u>,
   b) <u>Electrolysis</u>.
4) <u>Gold</u> is one of the few metals found as a <u>metal</u> rather than in a chemical compound (an ore).

## The Position of Carbon In the Reactivity Series decides it...

1) Metals <u>higher than carbon</u> in the reactivity series have to be extracted using <u>electrolysis</u>.

2) Metals <u>below carbon</u> in the reactivity series can be extracted by <u>heating the ore with carbon monoxide</u>.

3) This is obviously because carbon <u>can only take the oxygen</u> away from metals which are <u>less reactive</u> than carbon <u>itself</u> is.

Extracted using Electrolysis

Extracted by heating with carbon monoxide

| The Reactivity Series | |
|---|---|
| Potassium | K |
| Sodium | Na |
| Calcium | Ca |
| Magnesium | Mg |
| Aluminium | Al |
| CARBON | C |
| Zinc | Zn |
| Iron | Fe |
| Tin | Sn |
| Lead | Pb |

## Miners — they always have to get their ore in...

This page has four sections with three or four important points in each.
You need to practise <u>repeating</u> the details <u>from memory</u>. That's the <u>only effective method</u>.

# Extracting Iron

Iron is a very common element in the Earth's crust, but good iron ores are only found in a few select places around the world, such as Australia, Canada and Millom.

Iron is extracted from haematite, $Fe_2O_3$, by reduction (ie. removal of oxygen) in a blast furnace.

You really do need to know all these details about what goes on in a blast furnace, including the equations.

## The Raw Materials are Iron Ore, Coke and Limestone

1) The iron ore (haematite) contains the iron — which is pretty important.
2) The coke is almost pure carbon. This is for reducing the iron oxide to iron metal.
3) The limestone takes away impurities in the form of slag.

## Reducing the Iron Ore to Iron:

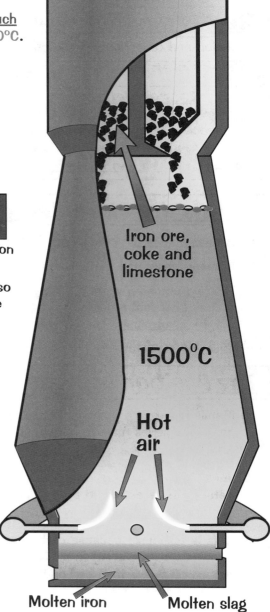

Iron ore, coke and limestone

1500°C

Hot air

Molten iron    Molten slag

1) Hot air is blasted into the furnace making the coke burn much faster than normal and the temperature rises to about 1500°C.

2) The coke burns and produces carbon dioxide:

$$C + O_2 \rightarrow CO_2$$
carbon + oxygen → carbon dioxide

3) The $CO_2$ then reacts with unburnt coke to form CO:

$$CO_2 + C \rightarrow 2CO$$
carbon dioxide + carbon → carbon monoxide

4) The carbon monoxide then REDUCES the iron ore to iron:

$$3CO + Fe_2O_3 \rightarrow 3CO_2 + 2Fe$$
carbon monoxide + iron(III)oxide → carbon dioxide + iron

The carbon monoxide itself combines with the oxygen in iron oxide to form carbon dioxide. This is OXIDATION.

5) The iron is of course molten at this temperature and it's also very dense so it runs straight to the bottom of the furnace where it's tapped off.

## Removing the Impurities:

1) The main impurity is sand (silicon dioxide). This is still solid even at 1500°C and would tend to stay mixed in with the iron. The limestone removes it.

2) The limestone is decomposed by the heat into calcium oxide and $CO_2$.

$$CaCO_3 \rightarrow CaO + CO_2$$

3) The calcium oxide then reacts with the sand to form calcium silicate or slag which is molten and can be tapped off:

$$CaO + SiO_2 \rightarrow CaSiO_3 \text{ (molten slag)}$$

4) The cooled slag is solid, and is used for:
   1) Road building    2) Fertiliser

## Learn the facts about Iron Extraction — it's a blast...

Three main sections and several numbered points for each. Every bit is important and could be tested in the Exam, including the equations. Use the mini-essay method for each section. Alternatively, cover it up one section at a time, and try repeating the facts back to yourself. And keep trying.

# Extracting Aluminium

Aluminium is extracted using <u>electrolysis</u> — which is a <u>chemical reaction</u> caused by electricity.

## A <u>Molten State</u> *is needed for* <u>Electrolysis</u>

1) <u>Aluminium</u> is <u>more reactive</u> than <u>carbon</u> so it has to be extracted from its ore by <u>electrolysis</u>.
2) The basic ore is <u>bauxite</u>, and after mining and purifying a <u>white powder</u> is left.
3) This is <u>pure</u> aluminium oxide, $Al_2O_3$, which has a <u>very high melting point</u> of over <u>2000°C</u>.
4) For <u>electrolysis</u> to work a <u>molten state</u> is required, and heating to 2000°C would be <u>expensive</u>.

## <u>Cryolite</u> *is used to* <u>lower the temperature</u> *(and costs)*

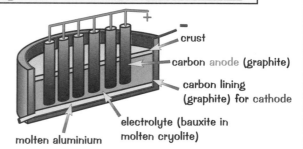

1) <u>Instead</u> the aluminium oxide is <u>dissolved</u> in <u>molten</u> <u>cryolite</u> (a less common ore of aluminium).
2) This brings the <u>temperature</u> needed <u>down</u> to about <u>900°C</u>, which makes it much <u>cheaper and easier</u>.
3) The <u>electrodes</u> are made of <u>graphite</u> (carbon).
4) The graphite <u>anode</u> (+ve) does need <u>replacing</u> quite often. It keeps <u>reacting</u> to form $CO_2$.

crust
carbon anode (graphite)
carbon lining (graphite) for cathode
electrolyte (bauxite in molten cryolite)
molten aluminium

## <u>Electrolysis</u> — *turning* <u>IONS</u> *into the* <u>ATOMS</u> *you want*

This is the <u>main object of the exercise</u>:

1) Make the aluminium oxide <u>molten</u> to <u>release</u> the aluminium <u>ions</u>, $Al^{3+}$ so they're <u>free to move</u>.

2) Stick <u>electrodes</u> in — so that the <u>positive</u> $Al^{3+}$ ions will head straight for the <u>negative electrode</u>.

3) At the negative electrode they just can't help picking up some of the <u>spare electrons</u> and "<u>zup</u>", they've turned into aluminium <u>atoms</u> and they <u>sink to the bottom</u>. This is called discharge.

Overall, this is a <u>REDOX reaction</u> and you need to know the <u>reactions</u> at both electrodes:

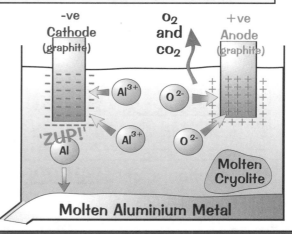

-ve Cathode (graphite)
$O_2$ and $CO_2$
+ve Anode (graphite)
$Al^{3+}$  $O^{2-}$
'ZUP!'
Al  $Al^{3+}$  $O^{2-}$
Molten Cryolite
**Molten Aluminium Metal**

### At the Cathode (–ve):

$$Al^{3+} + 3e^- \rightarrow Al$$
(<u>Reduction</u> — a gain of electrons)

### At the Anode (+ve):

$$2O^{2-} \rightarrow O_2 + 4e^-$$
(<u>Oxidation</u> — a loss of electrons)

## *Electrolysis is* Expensive — *it's all that* electricity...

1) Electrolysis uses <u>a lot of electricity</u> and that can make it pretty <u>expensive</u>.
2) Aluminium smelters usually have <u>their own</u> hydro-electric power station <u>nearby</u> to make the electricity as <u>cheap</u> as possible.
3) Energy is also needed to <u>heat</u> the electrolyte mixture to <u>900°C</u>. This is expensive too.
4) The <u>disappearing anodes</u> need frequent <u>replacement</u>. That costs money as well.
5) But in the end, aluminium now comes out as a <u>reasonably cheap</u> and <u>widely-used</u> metal. <u>A hundred years ago</u> it was a very <u>rare</u> metal, simply because it was so <u>hard to extract</u>.

## Electrolysis ain't cheap — well, there's always a charge...

Four main sections with several important points to learn for each. To start with you might find it easiest to cover the sections one at a time and try to <u>recall the details</u> in your head.
Ultimately though you should <u>aim to repeat it all in one go</u> with the whole page covered.

# *Purifying Copper*

1) Aluminium is a <u>very reactive metal</u> and <u>has</u> to be removed from its ore by <u>electrolysis</u>.

2) <u>Copper</u> is a very <u>unreactive</u> metal.  Not only is it below carbon in the reactivity series, it's also below <u>hydrogen</u>, which means that copper doesn't even react with <u>water</u>.

3) So copper is obtained <u>very easily</u> from its ore by <u>reduction</u> with <u>carbon</u>.

## <u>Very pure</u> Copper is needed for <u>Electrical</u> Conductors

1) The copper produced by <u>reduction isn't pure enough</u> for use in <u>electrical conductors</u>.

2) The <u>purer</u> it is, the better it <u>conducts</u>.  <u>Electrolysis</u> is used to obtain <u>very pure copper</u>.

The <u>cathode</u> starts as a <u>thin</u> piece of <u>pure copper</u> and more pure copper <u>adds</u> to it.

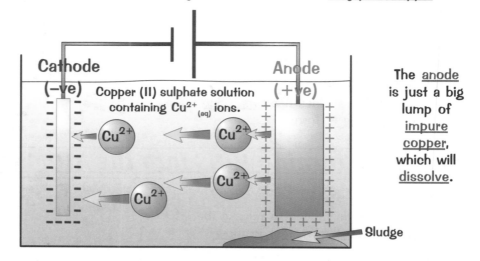

The <u>anode</u> is just a big lump of <u>impure copper</u>, which will <u>dissolve</u>.

### *Pure copper is deposited on the pure cathode (–ve)*

**The reaction at the _CATHODE_ is:**

$$Cu^{2+}_{(aq)} + 2e^- \rightarrow Cu_{(s)}$$

This is an example of <u>reduction</u>. The copper ions have been <u>reduced</u> to copper atoms by <u>gaining</u> electrons.

### *Copper dissolves from the impure anode (+ve)*

**The reaction at the _ANODE_ is:**

$$Cu_{(s)} \rightarrow Cu^{2+}_{(aq)} + 2e^-$$

Copper atoms have been <u>oxidised</u> into copper ions by <u>gaining</u> electrons. Overall, this is an example of a <u>REDOX</u> reaction.  Reduction and oxidation <u>can</u> <u>only</u> occur <u>simultaneously</u>.

The <u>electrical supply</u> acts by:

1) <u>Pulling electrons off</u> copper atoms at the <u>anode</u> causing them to go into the solution as <u>Cu²⁺ ions</u>.
2) Then <u>offering electrons</u> at the <u>cathode</u> to nearby <u>Cu²⁺ ions</u> to turn them back into <u>copper atoms</u>.
3) The <u>impurities</u> are dropped at the <u>anode</u> as a <u>sludge</u>, whilst <u>pure copper atoms</u> bond to the <u>cathode</u>.
4) The electrolysis can go on for <u>weeks</u> and the cathode is often <u>twenty times bigger</u> at the end of it.

## *Revision and Electrolysis — they both go on for weeks...*

This is a pretty easy page to learn.  The mini-essay method will do you proud here. Don't forget the diagram and the equations.   I know it's not much fun, but think how useful all this chemistry will be in your day-to-day life once you've learned it...
      ... hmmm, well... <u>learn it anyway</u>.

# Transition Metals

These are the transition metals

| | | | | | | | | | | | | | | | | | |
|---|---|---|---|---|---|---|---|---|---|---|---|---|---|---|---|---|---|

Sc | Ti | V | 52 Cr Chromium 24 | 55 Mn Manganese 25 | 56 Fe Iron 26 | Co | 59 Ni Nickel 28 | 64 Cu Copper 29 | 65 Zn Zinc 30

Here they are, right in the middle.

## 1) **They are** Chromium, Manganese, Iron, Nickel, Copper, Zinc

You need to know the ones shown in red fairly well. If they wanted to be mean in the Exam *(if!)* they could cheerfully mention one of the others like <u>scandium</u>, <u>titanium</u>, <u>vanadium</u> or <u>cobalt</u>. Don't let it hassle you. They'll just be testing how well you can "<u>apply scientific knowledge to new information</u>". In other words, just assume these "new" transition metals follow all the properties you've already learnt for the others. That's all it is, but it can really worry some folk.

## 2) Transition Metals **all have** high melting points **and** high density

They're <u>typical</u> metals. They have the properties you would expect of a proper metal:
1) <u>Good conductors</u> of heat and electricity.
2) Very <u>dense</u>, <u>strong</u> and <u>shiny</u>.
3) Iron melts at 1500°C, copper melts at 1100°C and zinc melts at 400°C.

## 3) Transition Metals **and their** compounds **make** good catalysts

1) <u>Iron</u> is the catalyst used in the <u>Haber process</u> for making <u>ammonia</u>.
2) <u>Manganese (IV) oxide</u> is a good catalyst for the decomposition of <u>hydrogen peroxide</u>.
3) <u>Nickel</u> is useful for turning <u>oils into fats</u> for making margarine.

## 4) **The** compounds **are very** colourful

1) The compounds are colourful due to the <u>transition metal ion</u> which they contain.
   eg:      Potassium chromate (VI) is <u>yellow</u>.
            Potassium manganate(VII) is <u>purple</u>.
            Copper (II) sulphate is <u>blue</u>.
2) The colour of people's <u>hair</u> and also the colours in <u>gemstones</u> like <u>blue sapphires</u> and <u>green emeralds</u> are all due to <u>transition metals</u>.

## 5) Transition metals **produce many** useful alloys

1) The transition metals can be easily <u>mixed</u> (when molten) to produce a <u>new</u> metal with different properties to the original metals. The new metal is called an <u>alloy</u>.
2) For example, the transition metals <u>zinc</u> and <u>copper</u> make the alloy <u>brass</u> for trumpets and tubas.

parp!

## Lots of pretty colours — that's what we like to see...

There's quite a few things to learn about transition metals. First try to remember the five headings. Then learn the details that go under each one. <u>Keep trying to scribble it all down</u>.

# Alkali Metals

They're called 'alkali metals' because their <u>hydroxides</u> dissolve in <u>water</u> to give an <u>alkaline</u> solution.   Simple.

## Learn These <u>Trends</u>:

As you go <u>DOWN</u> Group I,
the Alkali Metals become:

**1)** <u>Bigger atoms</u>

...because there's one extra full shell of electrons for each row you go down.

**2)** <u>More reactive</u>

...because the outer electron is more easily lost, because it's further from the nucleus.

**3)** <u>Higher density</u>

because the atoms have more mass.

**4)** <u>Even softer to cut</u> (they're all pretty soft)

**5)** <u>Lower melting point</u>

They have comparatively low melting points.

**6)** <u>Lower boiling point</u>

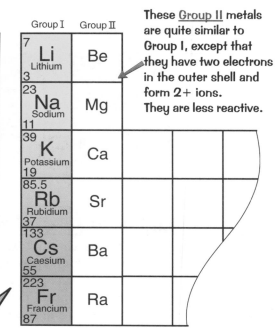

| Group I | Group II |
|---|---|
| 7 <br> **Li** <br> Lithium <br> 3 | Be |
| 23 <br> **Na** <br> Sodium <br> 11 | Mg |
| 39 <br> **K** <br> Potassium <br> 19 | Ca |
| 85.5 <br> **Rb** <br> Rubidium <br> 37 | Sr |
| 133 <br> **Cs** <br> Caesium <br> 55 | Ba |
| 223 <br> **Fr** <br> Francium <br> 87 | Ra |

These <u>Group II</u> metals are quite similar to Group I, except that they have two electrons in the outer shell and form 2+ ions.
They are less reactive.

## 1) <u>The Alkali metals are very</u> <u>Reactive</u>

They have to be <u>stored in oil</u> and handled with <u>forceps</u> (they burn the skin).

## 2) <u>They are:</u> <u>Lithium</u>, <u>Sodium</u>, <u>Potassium</u> <u>and a couple more</u>

Know those three names real well.  They may also mention Rubidium and Caesium.

## 3) <u>The Alkali Metals all have</u> <u>ONE outer electron</u>

This makes them very <u>reactive</u> and gives them all similar properties.

## 4) <u>The Alkali Metals all form</u> <u>1<sup>+</sup> ions</u>

They are <u>keen to lose</u> their one outer electron to form a <u>1<sup>+</sup> ion</u>.

## 5) <u>The Alkali metals always form</u> <u>Ionic Compounds</u>

They are so keen to lose the outer electron there's <u>no way</u>
they'd consider <u>sharing</u>, so covalent bonding is <u>out of the question</u>.

## 6) <u>Reaction with Cold Water produces</u> <u>Hydrogen Gas</u>

1) When <u>lithium</u>, <u>sodium</u> or <u>potassium</u> are put in <u>water</u>, they react very <u>vigorously</u>.
2) They <u>move</u> around the surface, <u>fizzing</u> furiously.
3) They produce <u>hydrogen</u>.  Potassium gets hot enough to <u>ignite</u> it.
   A lighted splint will <u>indicate</u> hydrogen by producing
   the notorious "<u>squeaky pop</u>" as the $H_2$ ignites.
4) Sodium and potassium <u>melt</u> in the heat of the reaction.
5) They form an <u>alkaline hydroxide</u> in solution, ie. <u>aqueous</u> $OH^-$ ions.

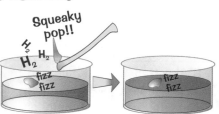

$$2Na_{(s)} + 2H_2O_{(l)} \rightarrow 2NaOH_{(aq)} + H_{2(g)}$$

$$2K_{(s)} + 2H_2O_{(l)} \rightarrow 2KOH_{(aq)} + H_{2(g)}$$

The solution becomes <u>alkaline</u>, which changes the colour of the pH indicator to <u>purple</u>.

## <u>Learn about Alkali Metals — or get your fingers burnt...</u>

Now we're getting into the seriously dreary facts section.  This takes a bit of learning.  <u>Enjoy</u>.

# Electrolysis of Salt

*Rocks and their Uses*

## Salt is taken from _the sea_ — and from _underneath Cheshire_

1) <u>Common salt</u> is a compound of <u>sodium</u> (an alkali metal) and <u>chloride</u> (a halogen).
2) It is found in large quantities in the <u>sea</u> and in <u>underground deposits</u>.
3) In <u>hot</u> countries they just pour <u>sea water</u> into big flat open <u>tanks</u> and let the <u>sun</u> evaporate the water to leave salt. This is no good in cold countries because there isn't enough sunshine.
4) In <u>Britain</u> (a cold country — as if you need reminding), salt is extracted from <u>underground deposits</u> left <u>millions</u> of years ago when <u>ancient seas</u> evaporated. There are massive deposits of this <u>rock salt</u> in <u>Cheshire</u>.

## Electrolysis _of Salt gives_ Hydrogen, Chlorine _and_ NaOH

Salt dissolved in water is called <u>brine</u>. When <u>concentrated brine</u> is <u>electrolysed</u> there are <u>three</u> useful products:

a) <u>Hydrogen gas</u> is given off at the cathode.
b) <u>Chlorine gas</u> is given off at the anode.
c) <u>Sodium hydroxide</u> is left in solution.

These are collected, and then used in all sorts of <u>industries</u> to make various products as detailed below.

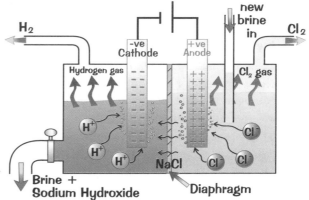

## Useful Products _from the_ Electrolysis of Brine

With all that effort and expense going into the electrolysis of brine, there'd better be some pretty useful stuff coming out of it — and so there is... and you have to learn it all too. Ace.

### 1) Hydrogen

1) Used in the <u>Haber Process</u> to make <u>ammonia</u> (see P.48).
2) Used to change <u>oils</u> into <u>fats</u> for making <u>margarine</u> ("hydrogenated vegetable oil"). Think about that when you spread it on your toast in the morning. Yum.

### 2) Chlorine

1) Used in <u>disinfectants</u>   2) Used to make <u>bleach</u>   3) Used for <u>killing bacteria</u>
(eg. in swimming pools)   4) Used for making <u>plastics</u>   5) Used to make <u>HCl</u>
6) Used to make <u>insecticides</u>

Don't forget the simple lab test for chlorine — it <u>bleaches</u> damp <u>litmus paper</u>.

### 3) Sodium hydroxide

Sodium Hydroxide is a very strong <u>alkali</u> and is used <u>widely</u> in the <u>chemical industry</u>.

eg: 1) <u>soap</u>   2) <u>ceramics</u>   3) <u>organic chemicals</u>   4) <u>paper pulp</u>   5) <u>oven cleaner</u>.

## Learn the many uses of salt — just use your brine...

There's not much to learn on this page so you've got no excuse for not <u>learning it all</u>. Write down where salt is found and the products from the electrolysis of brine, suggesting a few uses for each one. Believe me, you won't get much easier marks in the Exam than these. Giveaway.

*Rocks and their Uses*

# The Rock Cycle

Rocks shouldn't be confusing.  There are <u>three</u> different types: <u>sedimentary</u>, <u>metamorphic</u> and <u>igneous</u>. Over <u>millions</u> of years they <u>change</u> from one into another.  This is called the <u>Rock Cycle</u>.  Astonishingly.

## The Rock Cycle

1) Particles get washed to the <u>sea</u> and settle as <u>sediment</u>.

2) Over <u>millions</u> of years these sediments get <u>crushed</u> into <u>sedimentary rocks</u> (hence the name).

3) At first they get <u>buried</u>, but they can either <u>rise</u> to the surface again or they can <u>descend</u> into the <u>heat</u> and <u>pressure</u> below.

4) If they <u>do</u>, the heat and pressure completely <u>alter</u> the structure of the rock and they then become <u>metamorphic rocks</u> (as in "metamorphosis" or "change".  Another good name!).

5) These <u>metamorphic rocks</u> can either rise to the <u>surface</u> to be discovered by an enthusiastic geologist or else descend still <u>further</u> into the fiery abyss of the Earth's raging inferno where they will <u>melt</u> and become <u>magma</u>.

6) When <u>magma</u> reaches the surface it <u>cools</u> and <u>sets</u> and is then called <u>igneous rock</u>. ("igneous" as in "ignite" or "fire" — another cool name.  Gee, if only biology names were this sensible.)

7) When any of these rocks reach the <u>surface</u>, then <u>weathering</u> begins and they gradually get <u>worn down</u> and carried off to the <u>sea</u> and the whole cycle <u>starts over again</u>...  Simple, innit?

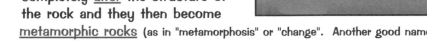

## Sedimentary Rocks form from Squeezed Layers

1) <u>Sedimentary rocks</u> are formed from <u>layers</u> of sediment deposited in <u>lakes</u> or <u>seas</u>.

2) Over <u>millions of years</u> the layers get buried under more layers and the <u>weight</u> pressing down <u>squeezes</u> out the water.

3) Fluids flowing through the pores deposit <u>natural mineral cement</u>.

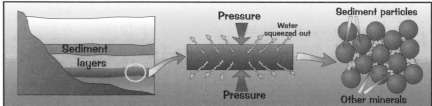

The two most common sedimentary rocks are <u>sandstone</u> and <u>limestone</u>.

## Fossils are mainly found in Sedimentary Rocks

1) Only <u>sedimentary</u> rocks (and some metamorphic rocks that were once sediments) contain <u>fossils</u>. The heat and pressure of <u>metamorphism</u> eventually destroys fossils.

2) Fossils are a very useful way of <u>identifying rocks</u> as being of the <u>same age</u>.

3) This is because fossilised remains that are found <u>change</u> (due to evolution) as the <u>ages pass</u>.

4) This means that if two rocks have the <u>same fossils</u> in, they must be from the <u>same age</u>.

## Rocks are a mystery — no, no, it's sedimentary my Dear Watson...

Don't you think the Rock Cycle is pretty ace?  Can you think of anything you'd rather do than go on a family holiday to Cornwall, gazing at the cliffs and marvelling at the different types of rocks and stuff?  Exactly.  (And even if you can, it's still a good plan to <u>learn about rocks</u>.)

*EDEXCEL MODULAR SYLLABUS*          *Module Nine — Chemicals and the Earth*

# Metamorphic and Igneous Rocks

## Heat and Pressure over Thousands of Years

Metamorphic rocks are formed by the action of heat and pressure on existing (sedimentary) rocks over long periods of time. You know that the rocks are changed versions of other rocks, because they have the same chemical compositions.

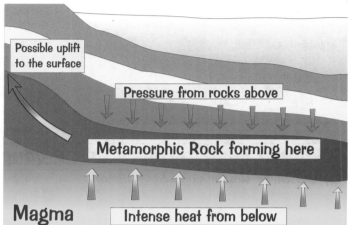

1) Earth movements can push all types of rock deep underground.

2) Here they are compressed and heated, and the mineral structure and texture may change but the composition stays the same. This is firm evidence that metamorphic rocks form from sedimentary rocks, eg. marble (metamorphic) and limestone (sedimentary) are both calcium carbonate.

3) So long as they don't actually melt they are classed as metamorphic rocks.

4) If they melt and turn to magma, they're gone. The magma may resurface as igneous rocks.

*Labels in diagram: Possible uplift to the surface; Pressure from rocks above; Metamorphic Rock forming here; Magma; Intense heat from below*

## Igneous Rocks are formed from Fresh Magma

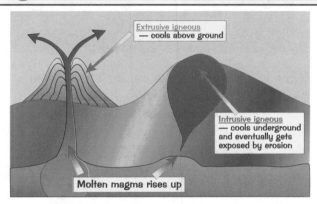

*Labels in diagram: Extrusive igneous — cools above ground; Intrusive igneous — cools underground and eventually gets exposed by erosion; Molten magma rises up*

1) Igneous rocks form when molten magma pushes up into the crust or right through it.

2) Igneous rocks contain various different minerals in randomly-arranged interlocking crystals.

3) There are two types of igneous rocks: EXTRUSIVE and INTRUSIVE:- and which type you get depends on how quickly the magma has cooled.

## INTRUSIVE igneous rocks cool SLOWLY with BIG crystals
## GRANITE is an intrusive igneous rock with big crystals

1) Granite is formed underground where the magma cools down slowly.
2) This means it has big randomly-arranged crystals because it cools down slowly.
3) Granite is a very hard and decorative stone ideal for steps and buildings.
4) Dartmoor is made of granite.

## EXTRUSIVE igneous rocks cool QUICKLY with SMALL crystals
## BASALT is an extrusive igneous rock with small crystals

1) Basalt is formed on top of the Earth's crust after bursting out of a volcano.
2) This means it has relatively small crystals — because it cooled quickly.

## Igneous Rocks are real cool — or they're magma...

It's very important that you know what granite looks like. You really should insist that "Teach" organises a field trip to see the famous pink granite coast of Brittany. About two weeks should be enough time to fully appreciate it. In May. Failing that, sit and learn this page in cold grey England.

# The Atmosphere

The Earth's atmosphere wasn't always as it is today. Here's how the first 4.5 billion years have gone:

## 1) Volcanoes gave out $CO_2$, $H_2$, $N_2$, Water Vapour and CO

**The First Billion Years**

1) The Earth's surface was molten for many millions of years. Any atmosphere boiled away.

2) Eventually it cooled and a thin crust formed but volcanoes kept erupting, releasing carbon dioxide ($CO_2$). The atmosphere probably also contained hydrogen ($H_2$), nitrogen ($N_2$), water vapour and carbon monoxide (CO).

3) The early atmosphere was mostly $CO_2$ (virtually no oxygen).

4) Holiday Report: Not a nice place to be. Take strong walking boots and a good coat.

## 2) Green Plants Evolved and Produced Oxygen

1) The water vapour condensed to form the oceans. Carbon dioxide dissolved into the oceans and consequently the levels of $CO_2$ dropped.

2) Over the next 2 billion years primitive plants evolved. As a result of photosynthesis, oxygen was released and the carbon dioxide levels were reduced.

3) Holiday Report: A bit slimy underfoot. Take wellies and lots of suncream.

**The Next 2 Billion Years**

## 3) Composition of the Air Today

**The Last Billion Years**

Nice safe balance

1) Over the last billion years or so, the atmosphere has evolved into what we know today.

2) Holiday Report: A nice place to be. Get there before the crowds ruin it.

| | | |
|---|---|---|
| 78% | Nitrogen | (Often written as 79% |
| 1% | Argon | Nitrogen for simplicity.) |
| 21% | Oxygen | |
| 0.04% | Carbon dioxide | |

Also :
1) Varying amounts of WATER VAPOUR.
2) And other noble gases in very small amounts.

# The Atmosphere is in a State of Approximate Balance

Different processes use and create oxygen and carbon dioxide at roughly the same rate nowadays, which results in a balanced atmosphere.

| USE OXYGEN AND CREATE CARBON DIOXIDE | USE CARBON DIOXIDE AND CREATE OXYGEN |
|---|---|
| 1) Respiration | 1) Photosynthesis turns carbon dioxide into oxygen. |
| 2) Burning of fossil fuels | 2) The oceans absorb some carbon dioxide. |

# Coo... 4½ Billion Years — just takes your breath away...

I think it's pretty amazing how much the atmosphere has changed. It makes our present day obsession about the $CO_2$ going up from 0.03% to 0.04% seem a bit ridiculous, doesn't it! Anyway, never mind that, just learn the three phases with all their details. You don't have to draw the pictures — although thinking about it, it's a pretty good way to remember it all. Yip.

# Reversible Reactions

*Useful Products from the Air*

A reversible reaction is one where the products can react with each other and convert back to the original chemicals. In other words, it can go both ways.

**A REVERSIBLE REACTION IS ONE WHERE THE PRODUCTS OF THE REACTION CAN THEMSELVES REACT TO PRODUCE THE ORIGINAL REACTANTS**

$$A + B \rightleftharpoons C + D$$

## Reversible Reactions will reach Dynamic Equilibrium

1) If a reversible reaction takes place in a closed system then a state of equilibrium will always be reached.

2) Equilibrium means that the relative (%) quantities of reactants and products will reach a certain balance and stay there. A 'closed system' just means that none of the reactants or products can escape.

3) It is in fact a dynamic equilibrium, which means that the reactions are still taking place in both directions but the overall effect is nil because the forward and reverse reactions cancel each other out.

The reactions are taking place at exactly the same rate in both directions.

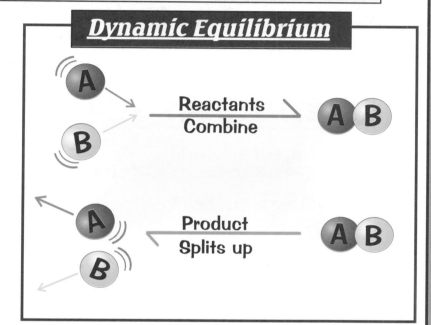

### Dynamic Equilibrium

Reactants Combine

Product Splits up

## Changing Temperature and Pressure to get More Product

1) In a reversible reaction the 'position of equilibrium' (the relative amounts of reactants and products) depends very strongly on the temperature and pressure surrounding the reaction.

2) If we deliberately alter the temperature and pressure we can move the "position of equilibrium" to give more product and less reactants.

### Two Very Simple Rules for Which Way the Equilibrium will Move

1) All reactions give out heat (they're exothermic) in one direction and take in heat (they're endothermic) in the other direction.
   If we raise the temperature the endothermic reaction will increase to use up the extra heat.
   If we reduce the temperature the exothermic reaction will increase to give out more heat.

2) Many reactions have a greater volume on one side, either of products or reactants.
   If we raise the pressure it will encourage the reaction which produces less volume.
   If we lower the pressure it will encourage the reaction which produces more volume.

## Learning/forgetting— the worst reversible of them all...

There's three sections here: the definition of a reversible reaction, the notion of dynamic equilibrium and two equilibrium rules. Make sure you can give a good rendition of all of them.

*Useful Products from the Air*

# The Haber Process

Ammonia is a good example of a 'useful product from the air'. Read on and find out how it's made.

## The Haber Process Makes Ammonia

1) The Haber process makes ammonia out of hydrogen and nitrogen.
2) The nitrogen is obtained easily from the air, which is 78% nitrogen (and 21% oxygen).
3) You don't need to know where the hydrogen comes from, so don't worry about it.
4) The Haber Process is a very important industrial process.
5) Ammonia is needed for making fertilisers, which are essential to modern farming.
6) Ammonia is also used to make nitric acid.

## The Haber Process is a Reversible Reaction:

$$N_{2\ (g)} + 3H_{2\ (g)} \rightleftharpoons 2NH_{3\ (g)} \quad (+ \text{ heat})$$

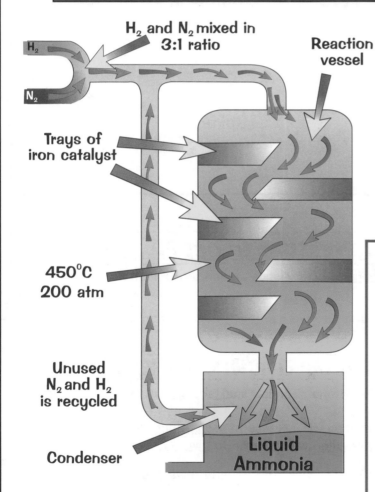

H₂ and N₂ mixed in 3:1 ratio

Reaction vessel

H₂

N₂

Trays of iron catalyst

450°C
200 atm

Unused N₂ and H₂ is recycled

Condenser

Liquid Ammonia

## Industrial conditions:

| PRESSURE: | 200 atmospheres |
| TEMPERATURE: | 450°C |
| CATALYST: | Iron |

Learn the industrial conditions off by heart — you could very easily be asked to give them in the Exam.

EXTRA NOTES:

1) The hydrogen and nitrogen are mixed together in a 3:1 ratio.
2) Because the reaction is reversible, not all of the nitrogen and hydrogen will convert to ammonia. The reaction reaches a dynamic equilibrium.
3) The ammonia is formed as a gas but as it cools in the condenser it liquefies and is removed.
4) The N₂ and H₂ which didn't react are recycled and passed through again so none is wasted.

## 200 atmospheres? — that could give you a headache..

There are quite a lot of details on this page. They're pretty keen on the Haber process in the Exams so you'd be well advised to learn all this. They could easily ask you any of these details. Use the same good old method: Learn it, cover it up, repeat it back to yourself, check, try again...

# The Haber Process Again

Here are some more important facts that you need to know about the wonderful Haber process.

## The Haber Process *is a controlled* Reversible Reaction

Here's the equation again:

$$N_{2\,(g)} + 3H_{2\,(g)} \rightleftharpoons 2NH_{3\,(g)}$$

## Higher Pressure *will Favour the* Forward Reaction *so build it strong...*

1) On the <u>left side</u> of the equation there are <u>four moles</u> of gas ($N_2 + 3H_2$), whilst on the <u>right side</u> there are just <u>two moles</u> (of $NH_3$).

2) So any <u>increase</u> in <u>pressure</u> will favour the <u>forward reaction</u> to produce more <u>ammonia</u>. Hence the decision on pressure is <u>simple</u>. It's just set <u>as high as possible</u> to give the <u>best % yield</u> without making the plant <u>too expensive</u> to build (it'd be too expensive to build a plant that'd stand pressures of over 1000 atmospheres, for example). The typical pressures used are 200 to 350 atmospheres.

## Lower Temperature WOULD *favour the forward Reaction BUT...*

The reaction is <u>exothermic</u> in the forward direction which means that <u>increasing</u> the temperature will actually move the equilibrium <u>the wrong way</u>, away from ammonia and more towards <u>$H_2$ and $N_2$</u>. <u>But they increase the temperature anyway</u>... this is the tricky bit so learn it real good:

**<u>LEARN THIS REALLY WELL:</u>**

1) The <u>proportion</u> of ammonia at equilibrium can only be increased by <u>lowering</u> the temperature.

2) But instead they <u>raise</u> the temperature and accept a <u>reduced</u> proportion (or <u>yield</u>) of ammonia.

3) The reason is that the <u>higher</u> temperature gives a much higher <u>rate of reaction</u>.

4) It's better to wait just <u>20 seconds</u> for a <u>10% yield</u> than to have to wait <u>60 seconds</u> for a <u>20% yield</u>.

5) Remember, the unused hydrogen, $H_2$, and nitrogen, $N_2$, are <u>recycled</u> so <u>nothing is wasted</u>.

## The Iron Catalyst *Speeds up the reaction and keeps costs down*

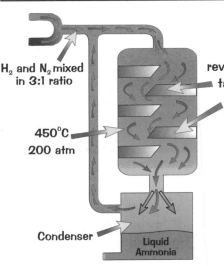

$H_2$ and $N_2$ mixed in 3:1 ratio

The actual reversible reaction takes place on the trays of iron catalyst

450°C
200 atm

Condenser

Liquid Ammonia

1) The <u>iron catalyst</u> makes the reaction go <u>faster</u> which gets it to the <u>equilibrium proportions</u> more quickly. But remember, the catalyst <u>doesn't</u> affect the <u>position</u> of equilibrium (ie. the % yield).

2) <u>Without the catalyst</u> the temperature would have to be <u>raised even further</u> to get a <u>quick enough</u> reaction and that would <u>reduce the % yield</u> even further. So the catalyst is very important.

3) <u>Removing product</u> would be an effective way to improve yield because the reaction keeps <u>chasing equilibrium</u> while the product keeps <u>disappearing</u>. Eventually <u>the whole lot</u> is converted.

4) This <u>can't be done</u> in the Haber Process because the ammonia can't be removed until <u>afterwards</u> when the mixture is <u>cooled</u> to <u>condense out</u> the ammonia.

## Learning the Haber process — *it's all ebb and flow...*

If they're going to use any reversible reaction for an Exam question, it'll probably be this one. The trickiest bit is that the temperature is raised not for a better equilibrium, but for speed. Try the mini-essay method to <u>scribble down all you know</u> about equilibrium and the Haber process.

*Useful Products from the Air*

# Fertilisers

Ammonium nitrate is a useful nitrogenous fertiliser that promotes growth in plants.

## Neutralise Ammonia to Make Ammonium Nitrate Fertiliser

Ammonium nitrate fertiliser can be made by neutralising ammonia with nitric or sulphuric acid.

This is a straightforward and spectacularly unexciting neutralisation reaction between an alkali (ammonia) and an acid. The result is of course a neutral salt: *(prod me if I fall asleep)*

$$NH_{3\,(g)} + HNO_{3\,(aq)} \rightarrow NH_4NO_{3\,(aq)}$$
Ammonia + Nitric acid → Ammonium nitrate

Ammonium nitrate is an especially good fertiliser because it has nitrogen from two sources — the ammonia and the nitric acid. Kind of a double dose. Plants need nitrogen to make proteins.

## Fertilisers Damage Lakes and Rivers — Eutrophication

1) Fertilisers which contain nitrates are essential to modern farming.

2) Without them crops wouldn't grow nearly so well, and food yields would be well down.

3) This is because the crops take nitrates out of the soil and these nitrates need to be replaced.

4) The problems start if some of the rich fertiliser finds its way into rivers and streams.

5) This happens quite easily if too much fertiliser is applied, especially if it rains soon afterwards.

6) The result is Eutrophication, which basically means "too much of a good thing". (Raw sewage pumped into rivers also causes eutrophication by providing food for microorganisms.)

7) Farmers need to take a lot more care when spreading artificial fertilisers.

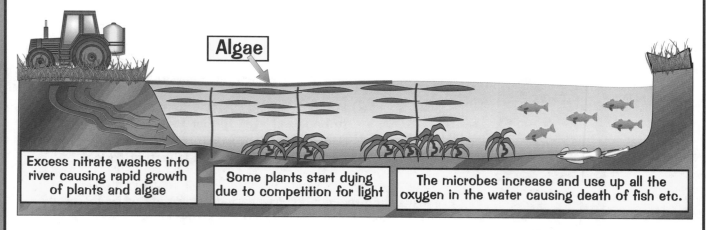

Excess nitrate washes into river causing rapid growth of plants and algae | Some plants start dying due to competition for light | The microbes increase and use up all the oxygen in the water causing death of fish etc.

As the picture shows, too many nitrates in the water cause a sequence of "mega-growth", "mega-death" and "mega-decay" involving most of the plant and animal life in the water.

## There's nowt wrong wi' just spreadin' muck on it...

Learn the equation for making ammonium nitrate out of ammonia and nitric acid. You could get asked about the dangers of using too much fertiliser. Learn all the numbered points and the diagram. A mini-essay is the best way to test yourself. Cover the page and scribble.

# The Noble Gases

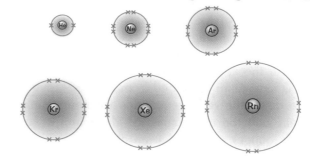

## As you go down the Group:

**1) The density** *increases*
 because the atomic mass increases.

**2) The boiling point** *increases*
 Helium boils at −269°C (that's cold!)
 Xenon boils at −108°C   (that's still cold)

## They all have *full outer shells*
### — That's why they're so *inert*

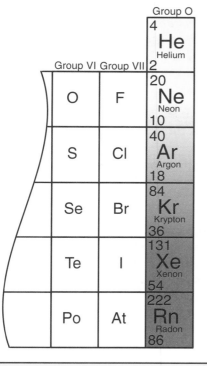

---

## HELIUM, NEON AND ARGON ARE NOBLE GASES

There's also <u>Krypton</u>, <u>Xenon</u> and <u>Radon</u>, which you may get asked about.
They're also sometimes called the <u>Inert</u> gases.  Inert means "doesn't react".

## THE NOBLE GASES DON'T REACT AT ALL

Helium, Neon and Argon don't form <u>any kind of chemical bond</u>
with anything.  They <u>always</u> exist as separate atoms. They won't even
join up in pairs.  The reason they are so unreactive is because they
have a <u>full outer shell of electrons</u> to start with.
Therefore they have no interest in losing or gaining any more electrons.

## HELIUM IS USED IN AIRSHIPS AND PARTY BALLOONS

Helium is ideal: it has very <u>low density</u> and <u>won't
set on fire</u> (like hydrogen does!).

## NEON IS USED IN ELECTRICAL DISCHARGE TUBES

When a current is passed through neon it gives out a bright light.

## ARGON IS USED IN FILAMENT LAMPS (LIGHT BULBS)

It provides an <u>inert atmosphere</u> which stops the very hot
filament from <u>burning away</u>.

## ALL THREE ARE USED IN LASERS TOO

There's the famous little red <u>Helium-Neon</u> laser
and the more powerful <u>Argon</u> laser.

---

# They don't react? — that's Noble De-use to us Chemists...

Well they don't react so there's obviously not much to learn about these. Nevertheless, there's
likely to be several questions on them so <u>make sure you learn everything on this page</u>.

# Revision Summary for Module Nine

*This section is pretty interesting stuff. Relatively speaking. Anyway, whether it is or it isn't, the only thing that really matters is whether you've learnt it all or not. These questions may not be entertaining, but they are the best way of finding out what you don't know. Don't forget — that's what revision is all about — finding out what you don't know and then learning it until you do.*

1) Describe the plus and minus points of iron (and steel), and give four uses for it.
2) Describe the plus and minus points of aluminium, and give four uses for it.
3) Name three useful properties of copper, and give three uses for it.
4) What are rocks, ores and minerals? Name a metal found as itself rather than an ore.
5) Give the chemical formula of iron ore.
6) What are the two methods for extracting metals from their ores?
7) What property of the metal decides which method is needed?
8) Draw and label a diagram of a blast furnace. What are the three raw materials used in it?
9) Write down the equations for how iron is obtained from its ore in the blast furnace.
10) How are the impurities removed from the iron? Give equations.
11) How is aluminium extracted from its ore? Give four operational details and draw a diagram.
12) Write down the redox equations for how aluminium is obtained from its ore.
13) Explain why the electrolysis of aluminium is so expensive.
14) How is copper extracted from its ore?
15) How is copper then purified, and why does it need to be?
16) Draw and label a diagram for the purifying process.
17) Where is the pure copper obtained?
18) Give the five physical properties of the transition metals.
19) List three uses of transition metals.
20) List four physical properties, and two chemical properties of the alkali metals.
21) Draw a *detailed, labelled* diagram showing *clearly* how brine is electrolysed.
22) Write down the three products of this electrolysis and write down uses for each of them.
23) What are the three types of rock? Draw a fully labelled diagram of the rock cycle.
24) Explain how the three types of rock change from one to another. How long does this take?
25) Draw diagrams to show how sedimentary rocks form.
26) What are found mainly in sedimentary rocks and sometimes in metamorphic rocks too?
27) How can fossils be used to identify rocks as being the same age?
28) Draw a diagram to show how metamorphic rocks are formed. What does the name mean?
29) Draw another diagram showing how igneous rocks are formed.
30) Name the two types of igneous rocks, and describe their properties.
31) How old is the Earth? What was it like for the first billion years or so?
32) What gases did the early atmosphere consist of?
33) What was the main thing which caused phase two of the atmosphere's evolution?
35) What is a reversible reaction?
36) Explain what is meant by "dynamic equilibrium" in a reversible reaction.
37) How does changing the temperature and pressure of a reaction alter the equilibrium?
38) What is the Haber process? What are the raw materials for it?
39) Draw a full labelled diagram for the Haber process and state the temperature and pressure used.
40) Explain the choice of pressure of the Haber process.
41) What determines the choice of operating temperature for the Haber process?
42) Give full details of how ammonia is turned into nitric acid, including equations.
43) What happens when too much nitrate fertiliser is put onto fields? Give full details.
44) What is the big fancy name given to this problem? How can it be avoided?
45) Name the noble gases.
46) Describe the change in properties of the noble gases as you go down the Group.
47) Give two uses for each of the first 3 noble gases.

## Atoms and Isotopes

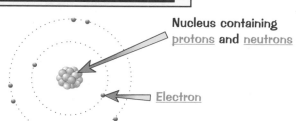

The structure of atoms is real simple.  I mean, gee, there's nothing to them.  Just learn and enjoy.

## Number of Protons Equals Number of Electrons

1)  Neutral atoms have no charge overall.

2)  The charge on the electrons is the same size as the charge on the protons but opposite.

3)  This means the number of protons always equals the number of electrons in a neutral atom.

4)  The number of neutrons isn't fixed but is usually just a bit higher than the number of protons.

Nucleus containing protons and neutrons

Electron

## Know Your Particles

Protons are Heavy and Positively Charged
Neutrons are Heavy and Neutral
Electrons are Tiny and Negatively Charged

| PARTICLE | MASS | CHARGE |
|----------|------|--------|
| Proton | 1 | +1 |
| Neutron | 1 | 0 |
| Electron | $\frac{1}{2000}$ | - 1 |

### THE MASS NUMBER

— Total of Protons and Neutrons

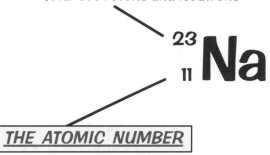

$^{23}_{11}\text{Na}$

### THE ATOMIC NUMBER

— Number of Protons only

### POINTS TO NOTE

1)  The atomic number tells you how many protons there are.  It's also known as the proton number.

2) This also tells you how many electrons there are.

3) The atomic number is what distinguishes one particular element from another.

4) All atoms of the same element have the same number of protons.

5) To get the number of neutrons — just subtract the proton number from the mass number.

6) The mass number is always the biggest number. It tells you the relative mass of the atom.

## Isotopes are the Same except for an Extra Neutron or two

You can't say what an isotope is.  You always have to start "Isotopes are...".  Learn this definition.

> ISOTOPES ARE:  different atomic forms of the same element, which have the SAME number of PROTONS but a DIFFERENT number of NEUTRONS.

1) The upshot is: isotopes must have the same atomic number but different mass numbers.

2) If they had different atomic numbers, they'd be different elements altogether.

3) A very popular pair of isotopes are carbon-12 and carbon-14.

**Carbon-12**  6 PROTONS
$^{12}_{6}\text{C}$    6 ELECTRONS
       6 NEUTRONS

**Carbon-14**  6 PROTONS
$^{14}_{6}\text{C}$    6 ELECTRONS
       8 NEUTRONS

## Just learn what those blinking numbers mean, OK...

I don't understand how people can get through the day without knowing this stuff, really I don't. Learn it now, and watch as the Universe unfolds and reveals its timeless mysteries to you.

## Elements and Compounds

*Chemical Bonds*

This page is 'elementary'. It's about 'compounding' your knowledge. (Sorry — I'll get my coat.)

## Elements *consist of* one type *of atom only*

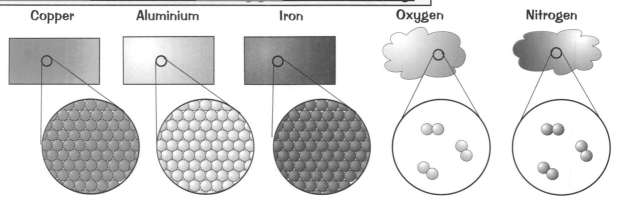

Copper        Aluminium        Iron        Oxygen        Nitrogen

## Compounds are Chemically Bonded

1) Carbon dioxide is a <u>compound</u> formed from a <u>chemical reaction</u> between carbon and oxygen.

2) It's <u>very difficult</u> to <u>separate</u> the two original elements out again.

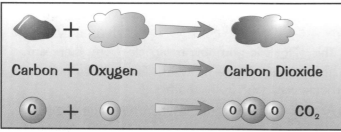

Carbon + Oxygen $\rightarrow$ Carbon Dioxide

C + O $\rightarrow$ O C O  $CO_2$

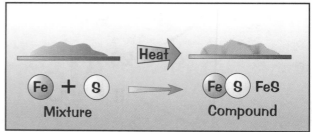

Fe + S $\rightarrow$ Fe S FeS
Mixture        Compound

3) The <u>properties</u> of a compound are <u>totally different</u> from the properties of the <u>original elements</u>.

4) If iron and sulphur react to form <u>iron sulphide</u>, the compound formed is a <u>grey solid lump</u>, and doesn't behave <u>anything like</u> either iron or sulphur.

## Water *and* Salt *are* Compounds

<u>Water</u> is a compound of <u>H</u>$_2$ and <u>O</u>$_2$ $\rightarrow$ <u>H$_2$O</u>

<u>Salt</u> or <u>Sodium Chloride</u> is a <u>compound</u> of sodium and chlorine. <u>Na</u> and <u>Cl</u>$_2$ $\rightarrow$ <u>NaCl</u>

Cl + Na $\rightarrow$ Cl Na
Chlorine + Sodium $\rightarrow$ Sodium Chloride

## Air is a Mixture of Gases

1) Don't confuse compounds with mixtures. A <u>mixture</u> consists of two or more elements or compounds <u>not chemically combined together</u>. The chemical properties of <u>each substance</u> in the mixture are <u>unchanged</u>.

2) Air is a <u>mixture</u> of gases. The oxygen, nitrogen, argon and carbon dioxide <u>can all be separated out quite easily</u>.

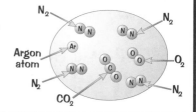

## Don't mix these up — it'll only compound your problems...

Elements, mixtures and compounds. To most people, they sound like basically the same thing. Ha! Not to GCSE Examiners they don't. You make mighty sure you remember their different names and the differences between them. <u>Just more easy marks to be won or lost</u>.

# Ionic Bonding

The fact that electrons occupy "shells" around the nucleus is what causes the whole of chemistry. Remember atoms much "prefer" to have full electron shells. It'll help you understand bonding.

## Ionic Bonding — Swapping Electrons

Ionic bonds form between metals and non-metals. Atoms lose or gain electrons to form charged particles (ions) which are then strongly attracted to one another (opposite charges attract).

## A shell with just one electron is well keen to get rid...

1) Atoms on the left hand side of the periodic table, such as sodium, potassium, calcium, have just one or two electrons in their outer shell.
2) They prefer full shells, so they're pretty keen to get shot of the extra electrons.
3) Given half a chance they do get rid, and that leaves the atom as an ion instead.
4) Ions tend to leap at the first passing ion with an opposite charge and stick to it like glue.

## A nearly full shell is well keen to get that extra electron...

1) Atoms on the right hand side of the periodic table (in Group Six and Group Seven), such as oxygen and chlorine, have outer shells which are nearly full.
2) They're obviously pretty keen to gain that extra one or two electrons to fill the shell up.
3) When they do they become ions.
4) Before you know it, POP, they've latched onto the atom (ion) that gave up the electron a moment earlier. The reaction of sodium and chlorine is a classic case:

The sodium atom gives up its outer electron and becomes an Na$^+$ ion.

The chlorine atom picks up the spare electron and becomes a Cl$^-$ ion.

# POP!

An ionic bond is formed.

## Giant Ionic Structures don't melt easily, but when they do...

1) Ionic bonds always produce giant ionic structures (eg. sodium chloride and magnesium oxide).
2) The ions form a closely packed regular lattice arrangement.
3) There are very strong chemical bonds between all the ions.
4) A single crystal of salt is one giant ionic lattice, which is why salt crystals tend to be cuboid in shape.

### 1) THEY HAVE HIGH MELTING POINTS AND BOILING POINTS

Due to the very strong chemical bonds between all the ions in the giant structure.

### 2) THEY DISSOLVE TO FORM SOLUTIONS THAT CONDUCT ELECTRICITY

When dissolved the ions separate and are all free to move in the solution, so obviously they'll carry electric current.

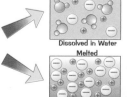

Dissolved in Water

Melted

### 3) THEY CONDUCT ELECTRICITY WHEN MOLTEN

When they melt, the ions are free to move and they'll carry electric current.

## Full Shells — it's the name of the game, pal...

Make sure you know exactly how and why ionic bonds are formed. There's quite a lot of words on this page but only to hammer home a few basic points. So learn them fast.

# Covalent Bonds

*Chemical Bonds*

## Covalent Bonds — Sharing Electrons

1) Sometimes atoms prefer to make <u>covalent bonds</u> by <u>sharing</u> electrons with other atoms.
2) This way <u>both</u> atoms feel that they have a <u>full outer shell</u>, and that makes them happy.
3) Each <u>covalent bond</u> provides one <u>extra</u> shared electron for each atom.
4) Each atom involved has to make <u>enough</u> covalent bonds to <u>fill up</u> its outer shell.
5) <u>Covalent bonds</u> are formed between <u>two non-metals</u> to form <u>molecules</u>. Learn these examples:

### 1) Hydrogen, $H_2$

Hydrogen atoms have just one electron. They <u>only need one more</u> to complete the first shell...

H—H

...so they form <u>single covalent bonds</u> to achieve this.

### 2) Chlorine, $Cl_2$

Chlorine bonds in the <u>same way</u> as <u>hydrogen</u>.

Cl—Cl

Each chlorine atom shares an electron and they <u>both</u> end up with full outer shells.

### 3) Hydrogen Chloride, HCl

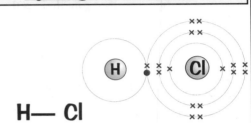

H— Cl

This is very similar to $H_2$. Again, both atoms need <u>one more electron</u> to complete their outer shells.

### 4) Oxygen Gas, $O_2$ and Water, $H_2O$

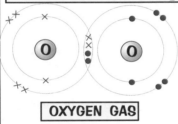

OXYGEN GAS

O=O

The <u>oxygen</u> atom has <u>six</u> outer electrons. Sometimes it forms <u>ionic</u> bonds by <u>taking</u> two electrons to complete the outer shell. However it will also cheerfully form <u>covalent bonds</u> and <u>share</u> two electrons instead, as in <u>oxygen gas</u> and <u>water molecules</u>, where it <u>shares</u> electrons with the H atoms.

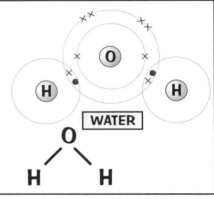

WATER

### 5) Methane, $CH_4$

Carbon has <u>four outer electrons</u>, which is a <u>half full</u> shell.

To become a 4+ or a 4– ion is hard work, so instead it forms <u>four covalent bonds</u> to make up its outer shell.

### 6) Carbon Dioxide $CO_2$

O=C=O

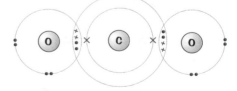

Carbon needs <u>four</u> extra electrons and oxygen needs <u>two</u>. So <u>two double bonds</u> are formed where two electrons from each atom are shared.

## Full Shells — you just can't beat them...

<u>Learn</u> the five numbered points about covalent bonds and the six examples. Then turn over and scribble it all down again. Make sure you can draw all six molecules perfectly and explain exactly why they form the bonds that they do. <u>All from memory of course.</u>

# Covalent Substances

*Chemical Bonds*

Substances formed from <u>covalent bonds</u> can either be <u>simple molecules</u> or <u>giant structures</u>.

## Simple *Molecular* Substances

1) The atoms form <u>very strong covalent bonds</u> to form <u>small molecules</u> of several atoms.
2) By contrast, the forces of attraction <u>between</u> these molecules are <u>very weak</u>.
3) The <u>result</u> of these <u>feeble inter-molecular forces</u> is that the melting points and boiling points are <u>very low</u>, because the molecules are <u>easily parted</u> from each other.
4) Most molecular substances are <u>gases or liquids</u> at room temperature.
5) Molecular substances <u>don't conduct electricity</u>, simply because there are <u>no ions</u>.
6) They <u>don't dissolve in water</u>, usually.
7) You can usually tell a molecular substance just from its <u>physical state</u>, which is always kinda "<u>mushy</u>" — ie. <u>liquid</u> or <u>gas</u> or an <u>easily-melted solid</u>.

Very weak inter-molecular forces

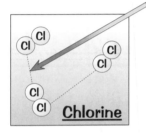
Chlorine

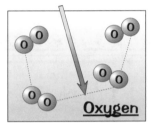
Oxygen

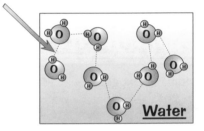
Water

## Giant Covalent *Structures*

1) These are similar to giant ionic structures except that there are <u>no charged ions</u>.
2) <u>All</u> the atoms are <u>bonded</u> to <u>each other</u> by <u>strong</u> covalent bonds.
3) They have <u>very high</u> melting and boiling points.
4) They <u>don't conduct electricity</u> — not even when <u>molten</u>.
5) They're usually <u>insoluble</u> in water.
6) The <u>main examples</u> are <u>diamond</u> and <u>graphite</u> which are both made only from <u>carbon atoms</u>.

### Diamond

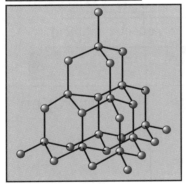

Each carbon atom forms <u>four covalent bonds</u> in a <u>very rigid</u> giant covalent structure.

### Graphite

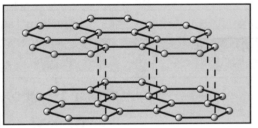

Each carbon atom only forms <u>three covalent bonds</u>, creating <u>layers</u> which are free to <u>slide over each other</u>, and leaving <u>free electrons</u>, so graphite is the only <u>non-metal</u> which <u>conducts electricity</u>.

### Silicon Dioxide

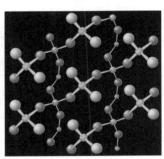

Sometimes called <u>silica</u>, this is what <u>sand</u> is made of. Each grain of sand is <u>one giant structure</u> of silicon and oxygen.

## Come on — pull yourself together...

There are two types of covalently bonded substances — and they're totally different. Make sure you know all the details about them and the examples too. <u>This is real basic stuff</u> — just easy marks to be won or lost... <u>Cover the page</u> and see how many marks you're gonna <u>WIN</u>.

## Chemical Equations

*Chemical Formulae*

Equations need a lot of practice if you're going to get them right.
They can get real tricky real quickly, unless you really know your stuff. Every time
you do an equation you need to practise getting it right rather than skating over it.

## Chemical Formulas **tell you** how many **atoms there are**

1) Hydrogen chloride has the chemical formula HCl. This means that in any molecule of
hydrogen chloride there will be: one atom of hydrogen bonded to one atom of chlorine.

2) Ammonia has the formula $NH_3$. This means that in any molecule of ammonia there will be:
three atoms of hydrogen bonded to one atom of nitrogen. Simple.

3) A chemical reaction can be described by the process reactants → products.
   eg. methane reacts with oxygen to produce carbon dioxide and water
   eg. magnesium reacts with oxygen to produce magnesium oxide.
You have to know how to write these reactions in both words and symbols, as shown below:

## The Symbol Equation **shows the atoms on both sides:**

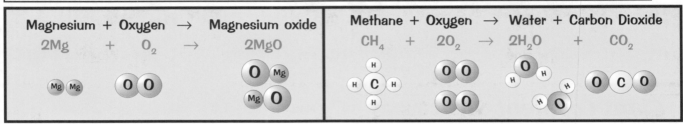

## You need to know how to write out any Equation...

You really do need to know how to write out chemical equations. In fact you need to know how to
write out equations for pretty well all the reactions in this book.
That might sound like an awful lot, but there aren't nearly as many as you think. Have a look.
You also need to know the formulae for all the ionic and covalent compounds in here too. Lovely.

## State Symbols **tell you what** Physical State **it's in**

These are easy enough, just make sure you know them, especially (aq) (in aqueous solution).

| (s) — Solid | (l) — Liquid | (g) — Gas | (aq) — Dissolved in water |

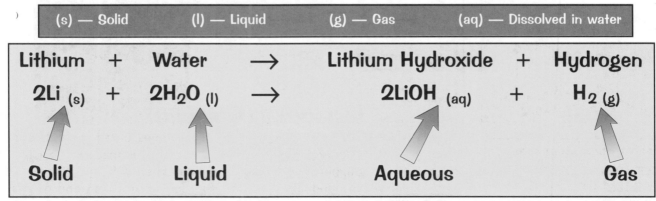

## It's tricky — but don't get yourself in a state over it...

Make sure you know the formulae for all the ionic and covalent compounds you've come across
so far. Try writing symbol equations for the following word equations and put the state symbols
in too:
   1) Iron (III) oxide + hydrogen →  iron + water
   2) Dilute hydrochloric acid + aluminium →  aluminium chloride + hydrogen.

# Balancing Equations

*Chemical Equations*

Things start to get a wee bit tricky now. Hang in there and remember... practice makes perfect.

## Balancing The Equation — match them up one by one

1) There must always be the <u>same</u> number of atoms on <u>both sides</u>, they can't just <u>disappear</u>.
2) You <u>balance</u> the equation by putting numbers <u>in front</u> of the formulae where needed.
   Take this equation for reacting sulphuric acid with sodium hydroxide:

$$H_2SO_4 \ + \ NaOH \ \rightarrow \ Na_2SO_4 \ + H_2O$$

The <u>formulae</u> are all correct but the numbers of some atoms <u>don't match up</u> on both sides. You <u>can't change formulae</u> like $H_2SO_4$ to $H_2SO_5$. You can only put numbers <u>in front of them</u>:

### Method: Balance just ONE type of atom at a time

The more you practise, the quicker you get, but all you do is this:

1) Find an element that *doesn't balance* and *pencil in a number* to try and sort it out.
2) *See where it gets you*. It may create *another imbalance* but pencil in *another number* and see where that gets you.
3) Carry on chasing <u>unbalanced</u> elements and it'll *sort itself out* pretty quickly.

<u>I'll show you</u>. In the equation above you soon see we're short of H atoms on the **RHS** (Right Hand Side).
1) The only thing you can do about that is make it $2H_2O$ instead of just $H_2O$:

$$H_2SO_4 \ + \ NaOH \ \rightarrow \ Na_2SO_4 \ + 2H_2O$$

2) But that now causes too many H atoms and O atoms on the **RHS**, so to balance that up you could try putting $2NaOH$ on the **LHS** (Left Hand Side):

$$H_2SO_4 \ + \ 2NaOH \ \rightarrow \ Na_2SO_4 \ + 2H_2O$$

3) And suddenly there it is! <u>Everything balances</u>. And you'll notice the Na just sorted itself out.

## Ionic Equations — make sure the electrons balance

Ionic equations are no different really, except that you have <u>electrons and charges</u> involved as well. The <u>total charge</u> on each side of the equation has to balance.

**Example:** The bond between sodium and chlorine in <u>sodium chloride</u> is ionic — a sodium atom gives a (negatively charged) electron to a chlorine atom. You can show this with <u>ionic equations</u>.

The sodium atom splits into a positive sodium ion and an electron...

$$Na \ \rightarrow \ Na^+ + e^-$$

$$Cl + e^- \ \rightarrow \ Cl^-$$

...and the chlorine atom gains the electron to become a negative chloride ion.

## You Need Ionic Equations for Electrolysis Reactions

Ionic equations are also used to describe what happens in <u>electrolysis</u>. Electrolysis is covered in full detail in <u>Module Nine</u>. Just for a laugh though, here are the ionic equations to show hydrogen and chlorine being given off during <u>electrolysis</u> of <u>sodium chloride</u> solution.

$H^+$ ions from water gain electrons to form hydrogen gas.

$$2H^+ + 2e^- \ \rightarrow \ H_2$$

$$2Cl^- \ \rightarrow \ Cl_2 + 2e^-$$

$Cl^-$ ions lose electrons to form chlorine gas.

## Balancing equations — weigh it up in your mind...

Practise scribbling down all these details, <u>mini-essay</u> style. This stuff can be a bit confusing, and I think you have to make a real effort to learn all the details. But seeing as they you're expected to know this stuff for any Chemistry module, it's the kind of thing you really <u>need to know</u>.

# Energy Transfer in Reactions

*Energy Transfers*

Whenever chemical reactions occur, energy is usually transferred to or from the surroundings.

## In an Exothermic Reaction, Heat is GIVEN OUT

An EXOTHERMIC reaction is one which gives out energy to the surroundings, usually in the form of heat and usually shown by a rise in temperature.

1) The best example of an exothermic reaction is burning fuels. This obviously gives out a lot of heat — it's very exothermic.

2) Neutralisation reactions (acid + alkali) are also exothermic.

3) Addition of water to anhydrous copper(II) sulphate to turn it into blue crystals produces heat, so it must be exothermic.

## In an Endothermic Reaction, Heat is TAKEN IN

An ENDOTHERMIC reaction is one which takes in energy from the surroundings, usually in the form of heat and usually shown by a fall in temperature.

Endothermic reactions are less common and less easy to spot. LEARN these three examples:

1) Photosynthesis is endothermic — it takes in energy from the sun.

2) Dissolving certain salts in water
   eg. 1) potassium chloride   2) ammonium nitrate

3) Thermal decomposition
   Heat must be supplied to cause the compound to decompose.
   The best example is converting calcium carbonate into quicklime (calcium oxide).

$$CaCO_3 \rightarrow CaO + CO_2$$

A lot of heat energy is needed to make this happen. The calcium carbonate has to be heated in a kiln and kept at about 800°C. It takes almost 30,000kJ of heat to make 10kg of calcium carbonate decompose.

## Energy Must Always be Supplied to Break bonds...
## ...and Energy is Always Released When Bonds Form

1) During a chemical reaction, old bonds are broken and new bonds are formed.
2) Energy must be supplied to break existing bonds — so bond breaking is an endothermic process.
3) Energy is released when new bonds are formed — so bond formation is an exothermic process.

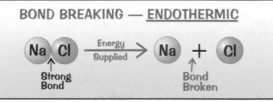

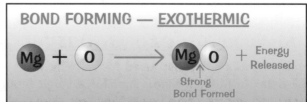

4) In an exothermic reaction, the energy released in bond formation is greater than the energy used in breaking old bonds.

5) In an endothermic reaction, the energy required to break old bonds is greater than the energy released when new bonds are formed.

## Exothermic and Endothermic — more lovely lingo...

Learn the numbered points until you know all the stuff. Usual tried and tested method.

# Relative Atomic Mass

Using Chemical Equations

The biggest trouble with relative atomic mass and relative formula mass is that they sound so bloodcurdling. "With big scary names like that, they must be really, really complicated." I hear you cry. Nope, wrong. They're dead easy. Take a few deep breaths, and just enjoy, as the mists slowly clear.

## Relative Atomic Mass, $A_r$ — easy peasy

1) This is just a way of saying how heavy different atoms are compared to each other.

2) The relative atomic mass $A_r$ is nothing more than the mass number of the element.

3) On the periodic table, the elements all have two numbers. The smaller one is the atomic number (how many protons it has). But the bigger one is the mass number (how many protons and neutrons it has) which, kind of obviously, is also the relative atomic mass. Easy peasy, I'd say.

Mass number
which is also
Relative Atomic Mass

$^4_2$He        $^{12}_6$C

Helium has $A_r$ = 4. Carbon has $A_r$ = 12. (So carbon atoms are 3 times heavier than helium atoms)

## Isotopes Affect the $A_r$ of an Element

The $A_r$ of an element is not always a whole number. It might seem confusing, but it's all to do with isotopes. Some elements consist of mixtures of two isotopes.

Chlorine has two isotopes

The Isotopes

$^{35}_{17}$Cl    $^{37}_{17}$Cl

The isotopes of chlorine have $A_r$ of 35 and 37. In any sample of chlorine, roughly 75% are chlorine 35, and 25% are chlorine 37.

So to work out the overall $A_r$ for chlorine we need an average atomic mass of the mixture of isotopes. For every atom of chlorine 37 there are three atoms of chlorine 35, so the $A_r$ of chlorine is given by:

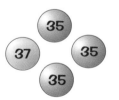

$$\frac{(3 \times 35) + 37}{4} = 35.5 \text{ (the } A_r \text{ of chlorine)}$$

Therefore the symbol for chlorine, as it appears in the periodic table is:     $^{35.5}_{17}$Cl

## Relative Formula Mass, $M_r$ — also easy peasy

If you have a compound like $MgCl_2$ then it has a relative formula mass, $M_r$, which is just all the relative atomic masses added together.
For $MgCl_2$ it would be:

$$MgCl_2$$
$$24 + (35.5 \times 2) = 95$$

So the $M_r$ for $MgCl_2$ is simply 95

You can easily get the $A_r$ for any element from the Periodic Table (see inside front cover), but in a lot of questions they give you them anyway.

## Phew, Chemistry — scary stuff sometimes, innit...

When you know it, cover the page and scribble down the important details. D'ya miss any?
1) Use the periodic table to find the relative atomic mass of these elements: Cu, K, Kr, Fe, Cl
2) Also find the relative formula mass of these compounds: NaOH, $Fe_2O_3$, $C_6H_{14}$, $Mg(NO_3)_2$

# Masses in Reactions

These can be kinda scary too, but chill out, little wide-eyed one — just relax and enjoy.

## The Three Important Steps — not to be missed...

(Miss one out and it'll all go horribly wrong, believe me)

1) **WRITE OUT** the balanced **EQUATION**
2) **WORK OUT** $M_r$ — just for the **TWO BITS YOU WANT**
3) Apply the rule: **DIVIDE TO GET ONE, THEN MULTIPLY TO GET ALL**
(But you have to apply this first to the substance they give information about, and *then* the other one!)

**EXAMPLE:** *What mass of magnesium oxide is produced when 60g of magnesium is burned in air?*

**ANSWER:**

1) **WRITE OUT THE BALANCED EQUATION:**

$$2Mg + O_2 \rightarrow 2MgO$$

2) **WORK OUT THE RELATIVE FORMULA MASSES:**

(don't do the oxygen — we don't need it)

$$2 \times 24 \rightarrow 2 \times (24+16)$$
$$48 \rightarrow 80$$

3) Apply the rule: **DIVIDE TO GET ONE, THEN MULTIPLY TO GET ALL**

The two numbers, 48 and 80, tell us that 48g of Mg react to give 80g of MgO. Here's the tricky bit. You've now got to be able to write this down:

> 48g of Mg ......reacts to give..... 80g of MgO
>
> 1g of Mg ......reacts to give.....
>
> 60g of Mg .....reacts to give......

**THE BIG CLUE** is that in the question they've said we want to burn "60g of magnesium" ie. they've told us how much magnesium to have, and that's how you know to write down the **LEFT HAND SIDE** of it first, because:

We'll first need to ÷ by 48 to get 1g of Mg
and then need to × by 60 to get 60g of Mg.

**THEN** you can work out the numbers on the other side (shown in orange below) by realising that you must **DIVIDE BOTH SIDES BY 48** and then **MULTIPLY BOTH SIDES BY 60**. It's tricky.

÷48 { 48g of Mg .............. 80g of MgO } ÷48
1g of Mg .............. 1.67g of MgO
×60 { 60g of Mg .............. 100g of MgO } ×60

You should realise that in practice 100% yield may not be obtained in some reactions, so the amount of product might be slightly less than calculated.

This finally tells us that 60g of magnesium will produce 100g of magnesium oxide.
If the question had said "Find how much magnesium gives 500g of magnesium oxide.", you'd fill in the MgO side first, because that's the one you'd have the information about. Got it? Good-O!

## Reaction Mass Calculations? — no worries, matey...

Learn the three rules in the red box and practise the example till you can do it fluently.
1) Find the mass of calcium which gives 30g of calcium oxide (CaO), when burnt in air.

# Empirical Formula

I've been around for a while and <u>not once</u> have I seen anyone die from too many formulae.
So you've got nothing to worry about. You can rest assured you'll live to the end of this page.

## Finding The Empirical Formula *(from Masses or Percentages)*

This sounds a lot worse than it really is. Try this for an easy peasy <u>stepwise method</u>:

1) <u>*LIST ALL THE ELEMENTS*</u> in the compound (there's usually only two or three!).
2) <u>*UNDERNEATH THEM*</u>, write their *EXPERIMENTAL MASSES OR PERCENTAGES*.
3) <u>*DIVIDE*</u> each mass or percentage <u>*BY THE*</u> $A_r$ for that particular element.
4) Turn the numbers you get into *A NICE SIMPLE RATIO*
   by multiplying and/or dividing them by well-chosen numbers.
5) Get the ratio in its *SIMPLEST FORM* — that tells you the formula of the compound.

**Example 1:** *Find the empirical formula of the iron oxide produced when 44.8g of iron react with 19.2g of oxygen. ($A_r$ for iron = 56, $A_r$ for oxygen =16)*

<u>Method:</u>

| | Fe | O |
|---|---|---|
| 1) *List the two elements:* | Fe | O |
| 2) Write in the *experimental masses:* | 44.8 | 19.2 |
| 3) *Divide by the $A_r$ for each element:* | $44.8/56 = 0.8$ | $19.2/16 = 1.2$ |
| 4) Multiply by 10... | 8 | 12 |
| ...then divide by 4: | 2 | 3 |

5) So the *simplest formula* is **2 atoms of Fe to 3 atoms of O**, i.e. $Fe_2O_3$. And that's it done.

I tell you what, since it's nearly Christmas, I'll run through another example for you:

**Example 2:** *Find the empirical formula when 2.4g of carbon reacts with 0.8g of hydrogen. ($A_r$ for carbon = 12, $A_r$ for hydrogen =1)*

<u>Method:</u>

| | C | H |
|---|---|---|
| 1) *List the two elements:* | C | H |
| 2) Write in the *experimental masses:* | 2.4 | 0.8 |
| 3) *Divide by the $A_r$ for each element:* | $\frac{2.4}{12} = 0.2$ | $\frac{0.8}{1} = 0.8$ |
| 4) Multiply by 10... | 2 | 8 |
| ...then divide by 2: | 1 | 4 |

5) So the *simplest formula* is **1 atoms of C to 4 atoms of H**, i.e. $CH_4$. That's Methane.

You need to realise (for the Exam) that this <u>empirical method</u> (ie. based on <u>experiment</u>) is the <u>only way</u> of finding out the formula of a compound. Rust is iron oxide, sure, but is it FeO, or $Fe_2O_3$? Only an experiment to determine the empirical formula will tell you for certain.

## *Old Dimitri Mendeleev did this sort of stuff in his sleep — the old rogue...*

Empirical formulae aren't half as bad as they sound. Make sure you <u>learn</u> those <u>5 steps</u> in the dark red box. Use them for every single empirical formula question you get.

# Revision Summary for Module Ten

*Another section over and a little bit wiser. Aha, but have you taken everything in? If you've learnt this module well enough, you'll manage these puzzlers without so much as a shrug. But if you get stuck, go back and have another squiz at the module. It's sure to sink in one day, and when it does you'll be thanking me for going on and on and on and on.*

1) Sketch any atom. Give two details about the nucleus.
2) What are the three particles found in an atom? What are their relative masses and charges?
3) What do the mass number and proton number represent?
4) Explain what isotopes are. Give a well-known example of an element with different isotopes.
5) What's the difference between elements, mixtures and compounds?
6) Give three examples each of elements, mixtures and compounds.
7) What is ionic bonding? Which kind of atoms like to do ionic bonding?
8) Why do atoms want to form ionic bonds anyway?
9) Which side of the periodic table has atoms with outer shells that are almost full?
10) Draw a diagram of a giant ionic lattice and give three features of giant ionic structures.
11) List the three main properties of ionic compounds.
12) What is covalent bonding? Which kind of atoms tend to do covalent bonding? Why is this?
13) Why do some atoms do covalent bonding instead of ionic bonding?
14) Are common molecules generally formed with covalent bonds? Do you get simple molecules
     with ionic bonds?
15) Draw diagrams and use symbols to illustrate the bonding in: $H_2O$, $HCl$, $CH_4$, $O_2$, $H_2$, $CO_2$.
16) What are the two types of covalent substances? Give three examples of each type.
17) Give three physical properties for each of the two types of covalent substance.
18) Diamond and sand are both very hard. How come?
19) Give three rules for balancing equations.
20) Balance these and put the state symbols in:
     a) $CaCO_3 + HCl \rightarrow CaCl_2 + H_2O + CO_2$     b) $Ca + H_2O \rightarrow Ca(OH)_2 + H_2$
     c) $H_2SO_4 + KOH \rightarrow K_2SO_4 + H_2O$          d) $Fe_2O_3 \rightarrow Fe + H_2O$
21) What's the difference between exothermic and endothermic reactions?
22) Give three examples of endothermic reactions.
23) How do you find out the relative atomic mass of an element?
     Write down the relative atomic mass of nitrogen.
24) Find Ar or Mr for these (use the periodic table inside the front cover):
     a) Ca   b) Ag   c) $CO_2$   d) $MgCO_3$   e) $Na_2CO_3$   f) ZnO   g) KOH   h) $NH_3$
     i) Sodium Chloride   k) Iron (II) chloride
25) Write down the three steps of the method for calculating reacting masses.
     a) What mass of carbon will react with hydrogen to produce 24.6g of propane ($C_3H_8$)?
     b) What mass of sodium is needed to produce 108.2g of sodium oxide?
     c) What mass of magnesium oxide is produced when 112.1g of magnesium burns in air?
26) What is meant by an empirical formula?
27) Work these out (using the periodic table):
     a) Find the EF for the iron oxide formed when 45.1g of iron reacts with 19.3g of oxygen.
     b) Find the EF for the compound formed when 227g of calcium reacts with 216g of fluorine.
     c) Find the EF for when 208.4g of carbon reacts with 41.7g of hydrogen.
     d) Find the EF for when 21.9g of magnesium, 29.3g of sulphur and 58.4g of oxygen react.

# Velocity and Acceleration

Forces and Motion

## Speed and Velocity are Both just how Fast you're Going

Speed and velocity are both measured in m/s (or km/h or mph). They both simply say how fast you're going, but there's a subtle difference between them which you need to know:

> SPEED is just how fast you're going (eg. 30mph or 20m/s) with no regard to the direction.
> VELOCITY however must also have the DIRECTION specified, eg. 30mph *north* or 20m/s, 060°.

Seems kinda fussy I know, but they expect you to remember that distinction, so there you go.

## Speed, Distance and Time — the Formula

$$\text{Speed} = \frac{\text{Distance}}{\text{Time}}$$

You really ought to get pretty slick with this very easy formula.
As usual the formula triangle version makes it all a bit of a breeze.
You just need to try and think up some interesting word for remembering the order of the letters in the triangle, s $^d$ t. Errm... sedit, perhaps... well, you think up your own.

Example:   A cat skulks 20m in 35s.  Find   a) its speed    b) how long it takes to skulk 75m.

Answer:    Using the formula triangle: a)  s = d/t = 20/35 = 0.57m/s
                                        b)  t = d/s = 75/0.57 = 131s = 2mins 11sec

A lot of the time we tend to use the words "speed" and "velocity" interchangeably.
For example to calculate velocity you'd just use the above formula for speed instead.

## Acceleration is How Quickly You're Speeding Up

Acceleration is definitely not the same as velocity or speed.
Every time you read or write the word acceleration, remind yourself: "acceleration is completely different from velocity. Acceleration is how quickly the velocity is changing."
Velocity is a simple idea. Acceleration is altogether more subtle, which is why it's confusing.

## Acceleration — The Formula

$$\text{Acceleration} = \frac{\text{Final Velocity} - \text{Initial Velocity}}{\text{Time Taken}}$$

Final velocity is often given the symbol $\underline{v}$ and initial velocity $\underline{u}$:
$$a = \frac{v - u}{t}$$

Well, it's just another formula. Just like all the others. Mind you, there are two tricky things with this one. First you need to work out the "change in velocity", as shown in the example below, rather than just putting in a simple value for speed or velocity.

Secondly there's the units of acceleration which are metres per second² (m/s²). Not metres per second (m/s), which is velocity, but m/s². Got it? No? Let's try once more: Not m/s, but m/s².

Example: A skulking cat accelerates from 2m/s to 6m/s in 5.6s. Find its acceleration.
Answer:  Using the formula:    a = (v–u)/t = (6 – 2) / 5.6  =  4 ÷ 5.6 = 0.71 m/s²
         All pretty basic stuff I'd say.

## Velocity and Acceleration — learn the difference...

It's true — some people don't realise that velocity and acceleration are totally different things.
Hard to believe, I know — all part of the great mystery and tragedy of life, I suppose.
Anyway. Learn the definitions and the formulae, cover the page and scribble it all down again.

Forces and Motion

# D-T and S-T Graphs

Make sure you learn all these details real good.  Make sure you can _distinguish_ between the two, too.

## Distance-Time _Graphs_

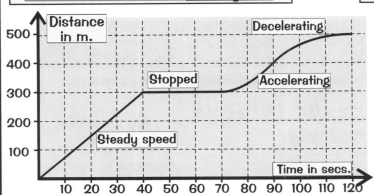

## Very Important _Notes_

1) _Gradient_ = speed.
2) _Flat_ sections are where it's _stopped_.
3) The _steeper_ the graph, the _faster_ it's going.
4) _Curves_ represent _acceleration_ or _deceleration_.
5) A _steepening_ curve means it's _speeding up_ (increasing gradient).
6) A _levelling off_ curve means it's _slowing down_ (decreasing gradient).

## _Calculating Speed_ **from a** _Distance-Time_ **Graph — it's just the** _Gradient_

For example the _speed_ of the _return_ section of the graph is:

Speed = gradient = $\frac{\text{vertical}}{\text{horizontal}}$ = $\frac{500}{30}$ = _16.7 m/s_

Don't forget that you have to use the _scales_ of the axes to work out the gradient.  _Don't_ measure in _cm_!

## Speed-Time _Graphs_

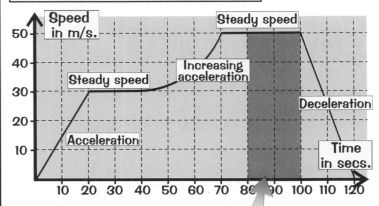

## Very Important _Notes_

1) _Gradient_ = _acceleration_.
2) _Flat_ sections represent _steady_ speed.
3) The _steeper_ the graph, the _greater_ the _acceleration_ or _deceleration_.
4) _Uphill_ sections (/) are _acceleration_.
5) _Downhill_ sections (\) are _deceleration_.
6) A _curve_ means _changing acceleration_.

The _distance travelled_ in any time interval is equal to the _area_.
For example, the distance travelled between t=80 and t=100 is equal to the _shaded_ area, which is equal to _1000m_.

_Higher_

## _Calculating_ Acceleration, Speed _and_ Distance _from a_ Speed-time _Graph_

1) The _acceleration_ represented by the _first section_ of the graph is:

Acceleration = gradient = $\frac{\text{vertical}}{\text{horizontal}}$ = $\frac{30}{20}$ = _1.5 m/s²_

2) The _speed_ at any point is simply found by reading the _value_ off the _speed axis_.

## _Understanding speed and stuff — it can be an uphill struggle..._

The tricky thing about these two kinds of graph is that they can look pretty much the same but represent totally different kinds of motion.  If you want to be able to do them (in the Exam) then there's no substitute for simply _learning all the numbered points_ for both types.  Enjoy.

# Stopping Distances For Cars

Forces and Motion

They're pretty keen on this for Exam questions, so make sure you learn it properly.

## The Many Factors Which Affect Your Total Stopping Distance

The distance it takes to stop a car is divided into the thinking distance and the braking distance.

### 1) Thinking Distance

"The distance the car travels in the split-second between a hazard appearing and the driver applying the brakes."

It's affected by three main factors:

a) How FAST you're going — obviously. It doesn't matter what your reaction time is, the faster you're going, the further you'll go.

b) How DOPEY you are — This is affected by tiredness, drugs, alcohol, reaction time and a careless attitude.

c) How BAD the VISIBILITY is — lashing rain and oncoming lights, etc make hazards harder to spot.

The figures below for typical stopping distances are from the Highway code. It's frightening to see just how far it takes to stop when you're going at 70mph.

### 2) Braking Distance

"The distance the car travels during its deceleration whilst the brakes are being applied."

It's affected by four main factors:

a) How FAST you're going — obviously. The faster you're going, the further it takes to stop.

b) The MASS of the vehicle — with the same brakes, a heavily-laden vehicle takes longer to stop. A car won't stop as quickly when it's full of people and towing a caravan.

c) How good your BRAKES are — all brakes must be checked and maintained regularly. Worn or faulty brakes will let you down catastrophically just when you need them the most, ie. in an emergency.

d) How good the GRIP is — this depends on three things:
1) road surface, 2) weather conditions, 3) tyres.

```
30 mph   50 mph   70 mph

9m       15m      21m

14m

6 car
lengths
          38m

          13 car    75m
          lengths

Thinking
distance

Braking              24 car
distance             lengths
```

Leaves and diesel spills and muck on t'road are serious hazards because they're unexpected. Wet or icy roads are always much more slippy than dry roads, but often you only discover this when you try to brake hard! Tyres should have a minimum tread depth of 1.6mm. This is essential for getting rid of the water in wet conditions. Without tread, a tyre will simply ride on a layer of water and skid very easily. This is called "aquaplaning" and isn't nearly as cool as it sounds.

## Muck on t'road, eh — by gum, it's grim up North...

They mention this specifically in the syllabus and are very likely to test you on it since it involves safety. Learn all the details and write yourself a mini-essay to see how much you really know.

Forces and Motion

# Newton's Laws of Motion

Around about the time of the Great Plague in the 1660s, a chap called <u>Isaac Newton</u> worked out the <u>Three Laws of Motion</u>. At first they might seem kind of obscure or irrelevant, but to be perfectly blunt, if you can't understand these <u>simple laws</u> then you'll never fully understand <u>forces and motion</u>.

## First Law — *Balanced Forces* **mean** *No Change* **in** *Velocity*

This first law was developed by <u>Galileo</u> and <u>Newton</u>, and is pretty straightforward:

> So long as the forces on an object are all *BALANCED*, then it'll just *STAY STILL*,
> or else if it's already moving it'll just carry on at the *SAME VELOCITY*
> — so long as the forces are all *BALANCED*.

1) When a train or car or bus or anything else is <u>moving</u> at a <u>constant velocity</u> then the <u>forces</u> on it must all be <u>balanced</u>.
2) Never let yourself entertain the <u>ridiculous idea</u> that things need a constant overall force to <u>keep</u> them moving — NO NO NO NO NO! This was what the <u>Greeks</u> used to think but it's <u>WRONG</u>.
3) To keep going at a <u>steady speed</u>, there must be <u>zero resultant force</u> — and don't you forget it.

<u>Steady Vertical Velocity</u> — Forces Balance (Weight force <u>equals</u> drag force).

<u>Steady Horizontal Velocity</u> — Forces Balance (Thrust force <u>equals</u> drag force).

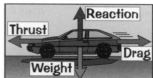

## Second Law — A *Resultant Force* **means** *Acceleration*

> If there is an *UNBALANCED FORCE*, then the object
> will *ACCELERATE* in that direction.

1) An <u>unbalanced</u> force will always produce <u>acceleration</u> (or <u>deceleration</u>).
2) This 'acceleration' can take <u>five</u> different forms:
   <u>Starting</u>, <u>stopping</u>, <u>speeding up</u>, <u>slowing down</u> and <u>changing direction</u>.
3) On a force diagram, the <u>arrows</u> will be <u>unequal</u>:

<u>Vertical Acceleration</u> — Unbalanced Forces (Weight force is <u>greater</u> than the drag force)

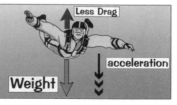

<u>Horizontal Acceleration</u> — Unbalanced Forces (Thrust force is <u>greater</u> than the drag force)

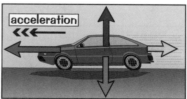

If the car <u>braked</u> the <u>resistance</u> force would be <u>larger</u> than the <u>driving</u> force — the car would <u>decelerate</u>.

<u>Don't ever say</u>: "If something's moving there must be an overall resultant force acting on it".

Not so. If there's an <u>overall</u> force it will always <u>accelerate</u>. You get <u>steady</u> speed from <u>balanced</u> forces. I wonder how many times I need to say that same thing before you remember it?

## Three Points **Which Should Be** Obvious

1) The bigger the <u>force</u>, the <u>greater</u> the <u>acceleration</u> or <u>deceleration</u>.
2) The bigger the <u>mass</u>, the <u>smaller the acceleration</u>.
3) To get a <u>big</u> mass to accelerate <u>as fast</u> as a <u>small</u> mass it needs a <u>bigger</u> force.
   Just think about pushing <u>heavy</u> trolleys and it should all seem fairly <u>obvious</u>, I would hope.

## *Hey, did you know — an unbalanced force causes ac...*

Key key key stuff here — it's well worth the effort reading through this page a couple of times until you've got it all. <u>Scribble</u> down what you can remember to check that you know it...

# Resultant Forces

## The Overall Unbalanced Force is called the Resultant Force

Any resultant force will produce acceleration and this is the formula for it:

$$F = ma \quad or \quad a = F/m$$

m = mass (kg), a = acceleration (m/s²)   F is always the RESULTANT FORCE (Newtons)

## Calculations using F = ma — Two Examples

Example:   What force is needed to accelerate a mass of 12kg at 5m/s² ?

Answer:     The question is asking for force — so you need a formula
with "F = something-or-other".
Since they also give you values for mass and acceleration,
the formula "F = ma" is a good choice, surely.

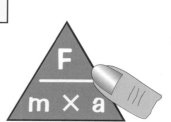

"F = ma" gives F = 12 × 5 = 60N.   (It's Newtons because force always is.)

(Notice that you don't really need to fully understand what's going on — you just need to know how to use formulae.)

## Resultant Force is Real Important — Especially for "F = ma"

The notion of resultant force is a real important one for you to get your head round — it's not especially tricky, it's just that it seems to get kind of ignored.

In most real situations there are at least two forces acting on an object along any direction. The overall effect of these forces will decide the motion of the object — whether it will accelerate, decelerate or stay at a steady speed. The "overall effect" is found by just adding or subtracting the forces which point along the same direction. The overall force is called the resultant force. When you use the formula "F = ma", F must always be the resultant force.

Example:   A car of mass of 1750kg has an engine which provides a driving force of 5,200N.
At 70mph the drag force acting on the car is 5,150N.
Find its acceleration:    a) when first setting off from rest    b) at 70mph.

Answer:     1) First draw a force diagram for both cases (no need to show the vertical forces):

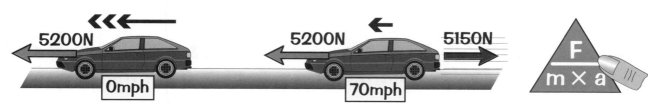

2) Work out the resultant force in each case, and apply "F = ma" using the formula triangle:

Resultant force = 5,200N
a = F/m = 5,200÷1750 = 3.0 m/s²

Resultant force = 5,200 – 5,150 = 50N
a = F/m = 50 ÷1750 = 0.03 m/s²

## Newton — what I'd give to drop an apple on him...

Newton's second law is one of the key ideas in Physics — it's almost certain to be on your Exam. Learn the formula, and especially how to use it from the examples above.

**Forces and Motion**

# Reaction Forces

## The Third Law — *Reaction Forces*

> If object A *EXERTS A FORCE* on object B
> then object B exerts *THE EXACT OPPOSITE FORCE* on object A.

1) That means if you <u>push</u> against a wall, the wall will <u>push back</u>, <u>just as hard</u>.
2) And as soon as you <u>stop</u> pushing, <u>so does the wall</u>. Kinda clever really.
3) If you think about it, there must be an <u>opposing force</u> when you lean against a wall — otherwise you (and the wall) would <u>fall over</u>.
4) If you <u>pull</u> a cart, whatever force <u>you exert</u> on the rope, the rope exerts the <u>exact opposite</u> pull on <u>you</u>.
5) If you put a book on a table, the <u>weight</u> of the book acts <u>downwards</u> on the table — and the table exerts an <u>equal and opposite</u> force <u>upwards</u> on the book.
6) If you support a book on your <u>hand</u>, the book exerts its <u>weight</u> downwards on you, and you provide an <u>upwards</u> force on the book and it all stays nicely <u>in balance</u>.

> Whenever an object is on a horizontal *SURFACE*, there'll always be a *REACTION FORCE* pushing *UPWARDS*, supporting the object. The total *REACTION FORCE* will be *EQUAL AND OPPOSITE* to the weight.

## *Gravitational* **attraction**

It's that guy again — <u>Isaac Newton.</u> This time he worked out that there's <u>gravitational attraction</u> between <u>all</u> masses. This has <u>two</u> important effects:
1) It makes all things <u>accelerate</u> towards the <u>ground</u> (<u>WITHOUT AIR</u> everything has the <u>same</u> acceleration — $10\text{m/s}^2$ on Earth).
2) It gives everything a <u>weight</u>.

## *Weight* **and** *Mass* **are** *Not the Same*

To understand this you must learn <u>all</u> these facts about <u>mass</u> and <u>weight</u>.
1) <u>Mass</u> is the <u>amount of matter</u> in an object. For any given object this will have the same value <u>anywhere</u> in the Universe.
2) <u>Weight</u> is caused by the <u>pull</u> of gravity. In most questions the <u>weight</u> of an object is just the <u>force</u> of gravity pulling it towards the centre of the <u>Earth</u>.
3) An object has the <u>same mass</u> whether it's on Earth or the Moon — but its <u>weight</u> will be <u>different</u>. A 1kg mass will <u>weigh less on the moon</u> (1.6N) than it does on Earth (10N) simply because the <u>force of gravity</u> pulling on it is less.
4) Weight is a <u>force</u> measured in Newtons. It's measured with a <u>spring balance</u> or Newton meter.

> <u>ONE NEWTON</u> is the force needed to give a MASS OF 1 kg an *ACCELERATION OF* $1\text{m/s}^2$.

## **The** *Very Important Formula* **relating** *Mass, Weight* **and** *Gravity*

$$W = m \times g$$

(Weight = mass × g)

1) Remember, weight and mass are <u>not the same</u>. Mass is in <u>kg</u>, weight is in <u>Newtons</u>.
2) The letter "g" represents the <u>strength</u> of the gravity and its value is <u>different</u> for <u>different planets</u>. <u>On Earth</u> g ≈ 10 N/kg. <u>On the moon</u>, where the gravity is weaker, g is just 1.6 N/kg.

## *We're all attracted to each other — physically at least...*

In <u>Exam</u> questions they may well <u>test</u> you on <u>reaction forces</u>, by getting you to label diagrams with arrows. Make sure you learn the <u>diagrams</u> on this page real well, keep trying till you know them all...

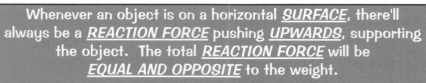

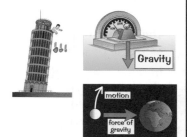

# Force diagrams

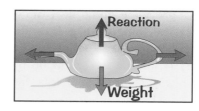

Forces and Motion

There are basically only a few <u>different force diagrams</u> you can get, so learn all of them...

## Force **Diagrams**

### 1) *Stationary Object* — **All Forces in** Balance

1) The force of <u>Gravity</u> (or weight) is acting <u>downwards</u>.
2) This causes a <u>reaction force</u> from the surface <u>pushing</u> the object <u>back up</u>.
3) <u>Without</u> a reaction force, it would accelerate <u>downwards</u> due to the pull of gravity.
4) The two <u>horizontal forces</u> must be <u>equal and opposite</u> — otherwise the object will accelerate <u>sideways</u>.

Equal and opposite forces

### 2) *Steady Velocity* — **All Forces in** Balance*!*

<u>Take note</u>! To move with a <u>steady speed</u> the forces must be in <u>balance</u>. If there is an <u>unbalanced force</u> then you get <u>acceleration</u>, not steady speed. That's <u>rrrreal important</u> so don't forget it.

### 3) *Acceleration* — **Unbalanced** Forces

1) You only get <u>acceleration</u> with an overall <u>resultant</u> (unbalanced) <u>force</u>.
2) The <u>bigger</u> this <u>unbalanced force</u>, the <u>greater</u> the <u>acceleration</u>.
3) Note that the forces in the <u>other direction</u> are still <u>balanced</u>.

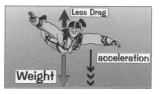

# Cars **and** Free-Fallers **all Reach a** Terminal Velocity

1) When cars and free-falling objects first <u>set off</u> they have <u>much more</u> force <u>accelerating</u> them than <u>resistance</u> slowing them down.
2) As the <u>speed</u> increases the resistance <u>builds up</u>.
3) This gradually <u>reduces</u> the <u>acceleration</u> until eventually the <u>resistance force</u> is <u>equal</u> to the <u>accelerating force</u> and then it won't be able to accelerate any more.
4) It will have reached its maximum speed or <u>TERMINAL VELOCITY</u>.

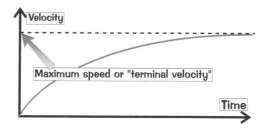

1) The most important example is the human <u>skydiver</u>.
2) Without his parachute open there is a force of "W=mg" pulling him down but little <u>resistance</u>.
3) He reaches a <u>terminal velocity</u> of about <u>120mph</u> — when the <u>force of air resistance equals his weight</u>.
4) But with the parachute <u>open</u>, there's much more <u>air resistance</u> and still only the same force "W=mg" pulling him down.
5) This means his <u>terminal velocity</u> comes right down to about <u>15mph</u>, which is a <u>safe speed</u> to hit the ground at.

## *Learning about air resistance — it can be a real drag...*

It looks like mini-essay time to me. There's a lot of details swirling around here, so definitely the best way of checking how much you know is to <u>scribble down a mini-essay</u> for each of the three sections. Then <u>check back</u> and see what you <u>missed</u>. Then try again. <u>And keep trying</u>.

Forces and Energy

# Work and Power

## When a force moves an object, energy is transferred and work is done.

That statement sounds far more complicated than it needs to.  Try this:

1) Whenever something moves, something else is providing some sort of "effort" to move it.
2) The thing putting the effort in needs a supply of energy (like fuel or food or electricity etc.).
3) It then does "work" by moving the object — and one way or another it transfers the energy it receives (as fuel) into other forms.
4) Whether this energy is transferred 'usefully' (eg. by lifting a load) or is 'wasted' (lost as friction), you can still say that work is done.  Just like Batman and Bruce Wayne, work done and energy transferred are indeed one and the same.  (And they're both in Joules)

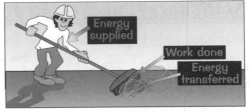

## It's Just Another Trivial Formula

### Work Done = Force × Distance

Whether the force is friction or weight or tension in a rope, it's always the same.  To find how much energy has been transferred (in Joules), you just multiply the force (in N) by the distance moved in the direction of the force (in m).  Easy as that.  I'll show you...

Example:  Some hooligan kids drag an old tractor tyre 5m over rough ground.  They pull with a total force of 340N.  Find the energy transferred.

Answer:  Wd = F×d = 340 × 5 = 1700J.   Phew — easy peasy isn't it?

## Power is the "Rate of Doing Work" — ie. how much per second

Power is not the same thing as force, nor energy.  A powerful machine is not necessarily one which can exert a strong force (though it usually ends up that way).
A powerful machine is one which transfers a lot of energy in a short space of time.
This is the very easy formula for power:

$$\text{Power} = \frac{\text{Work done}}{\text{Time taken}}$$

Example:  A motor transfers 4.8kJ of useful energy in 2 minutes.  Find its power output.
Answer:  P = Wd / t = 4,800/120 = 40W (or 40 J/s).
(Note that the kJ had to be turned into J, and the minutes into seconds.)

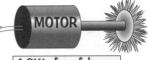

4.8KJ of useful energy in 2 minutes

## Power is Measured in Watts (or J/s)

The proper unit of power is the Watt.  One Watt = 1 Joule of energy transferred per second.
Power means "how much energy per second", so Watts are the same as "Joules per second" (J/s).
Don't ever say "Watts per second" — it's nonsense.

## Revise work done — force yourself to go the distance...

"Energy transferred" and "work done" are the same thing.  I wonder how many times I need to say that before you'll remember.   Power is "work done divided by time taken".  I wonder how many times you've got to see that before you realise you're supposed to learn it as well...

# Kinetic and Potential Energy

Forces and Energy

## Kinetic Energy *is Energy of* Movement

Kinetic energy is movement energy. There's a slightly tricky formula for it, so you have to concentrate a little bit harder for this one. But hey, that's life — it can be real tough sometimes:

## Kinetic Energy = ½ × mass × velocity²

Example: A car of mass 2450kg is travelling at 38m/s. Calculate its kinetic energy.

Answer: It's pretty easy. You just plug the numbers into the formula but watch the "v²" (m/s)². KE = ½mv² = ½ × 2450 × 38² = <u>1 768 900 J</u> (Joules because it's energy).
(When the car stops suddenly, all this energy is dissipated as heat at the brakes — it's a lot of heat)

Remember, the kinetic energy of something depends both on <u>MASS</u> and <u>SPEED</u>. The more it weighs and the faster it's going, the bigger its kinetic energy will be.

small mass, not fast low kinetic energy

big fast lorries Ltd

big mass, real fast high kinetic energy

## Potential Energy *is Energy* Due to Height

The proper name for this kind of "Potential Energy" is Gravitational Potential Energy, (as opposed to "elastic potential energy" or "chemical potential energy"). The proper name for g is "gravitational field strength". On Earth this has the value of <u>g = 10m/s²</u>.

## Potential Energy = mass × g × height

Example: A sheep of mass 47kg is raised through 6.3m. Find the gain in potential energy.
Answer: It's even easier than before. You just plug the numbers into the formula:
P.E. = mgh = 47 × 10 × 6.3 = <u>2961 J</u> (Joules because it's energy).

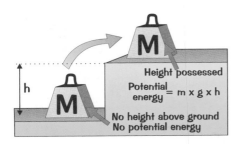

Strictly speaking it's the <u>change</u> in potential energy we're dealing with, so the formula can sometimes be written as: "<u>CHANGE</u> in Potential Energy = mass × g × <u>CHANGE</u> in height".
But that's a minor detail really, because it all works out just the same anyway.

## Kinetic Energy — *just get a move on and learn it, OK...*

Phew! A couple of tricky formulae for you here. I mean, gosh they've got more than three letters in them. Still, at least they fit into formula triangles, so you may still have some small chance of getting them right. Come on, I'm joking. Formulae are always <u>a doddle</u> aren't they?

# Seismic Waves

*Earth Waves*

## Seismic Waves <u>are caused by</u> Earthquakes

1) We can only drill <u>about 10km</u> or so into the crust of the Earth, which is not very far, so <u>seismic waves</u> are really the <u>only</u> way of investigating the <u>inner structure</u>.
2) When there's an <u>Earthquake</u> or <u>Underground Explosion</u> somewhere the <u>seismic waves</u> travel out from it and we <u>detect</u> them all over the surface of the planet using <u>seismographs</u>.
3) We measure the <u>time</u> it takes for the <u>two</u> different types of shock wave to reach each <u>seismograph</u>.
4) We also note the parts of the Earth which <u>don't</u> receive the shock waves at all.
5) From this information you can work out <u>all sorts</u> of stuff about the inside of the Earth as shown below:

## Different Waves <u>Take</u> Different Paths

### Longitudinal <u>Waves</u>

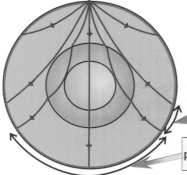

<u>Longitudinal Waves</u> travel through both <u>solids</u> and <u>liquids</u>. They travel <u>faster</u> than <u>transverse</u> waves.

No Longitudinal waves reach here

Longitudinal waves pass through core and are detected here

### Transverse <u>Waves</u>

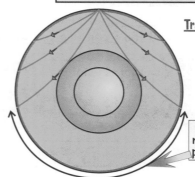

<u>Transverse Waves</u> will <u>only</u> travel through <u>solids</u>.

No Transverse waves reach here, they can't pass through the core

## The <u>Seismograph</u> Results Tell Us What's <u>Down There</u>

1) About <u>halfway through</u> the Earth, there's an <u>abrupt change in direction</u> of both types of wave. This indicates that there's a <u>sudden change in properties</u> at that point — the <u>core</u>.
2) The fact that transverse waves are <u>not detected</u> in the <u>shadow</u> of this core tells us that it's <u>liquid</u>.
3) It's also found that <u>longitudinal waves</u> travel <u>slightly faster</u> through the <u>middle</u> of the core, which strongly suggests that there's a <u>solid inner core</u>.
4) Note that <u>transverse waves</u> do travel through the <u>mantle</u>, which shows that it's <u>solid</u>. It only melts to form magma in small 'hot spots'.

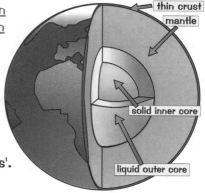

thin crust
mantle
solid inner core
liquid outer core

## The Paths <u>Curve with</u> Increasing Depth

1) The <u>waves</u> change speed as the <u>properties</u> of the mantle and core change.
2) This change in speed causes the waves to change direction — which is <u>refraction</u>, of course.
3) Most of the time the waves change speed <u>gradually</u>, resulting in a <u>curved</u> path.
4) But when the properties change suddenly, the speed will change abruptly, and the path will have a kink.

## Seismic Waves — they reveal the terrible trembling truth...

Once again there are four main sections to learn. <u>Learn</u> the headings first, then try <u>scribbling down</u> all the details for each heading, including the diagrams. Make an extra effort to remember the differences between <u>longitudinal</u> and <u>transverse</u> waves.

*Higher*  *Higher*  *Higher*  *Higher*

# Plates and Boundaries

*Earth Waves*

## The Earth's Surface is made up of Large Plates of Rock

1) The Earth's lithosphere is the crust and the upper part of the mantle. It's cracked into pieces called tectonic plates.
2) These plates are like big rafts that float across the mantle.
3) The map shows the edges of these plates. As they move, the continents move too.
4) The plates are moving at a speed of about 1cm or 2cm per year.

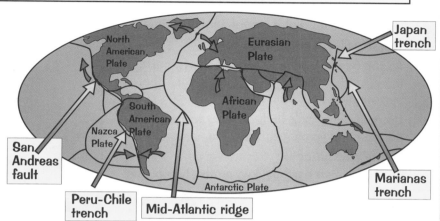

## Tectonic Plate Boundaries

At the boundaries between tectonic plates there's usually trouble like volcanoes or earthquakes. There are three different ways that plates interact: colliding, separating or sliding past each other.

## Plates Sliding Past Each Other: San Francisco

1) Sometimes the plates are just sliding past each other.
2) The best known example of this is the San Andreas Fault in California.
3) A narrow strip of the coastline is sliding north at about 7cm a year.
4) The rock plates don't glide smoothly past each other.
5) They catch and deform each other and as the forces build up they suddenly lurch.
6) This sudden lurching only lasts a few seconds — but it'll bring buildings down, no problem.
7) The city of San Francisco sits astride this fault line. (They didn't know that when they built it!)
8) The city was destroyed by an earthquake in 1906 and hit by another quite serious one in 1989. They could have another one any time.
9) In earthquake zones they try to build earthquake-proof buildings which are designed to withstand a bit of shaking.
10) Earthquakes usually cause much greater devastation in poorer countries where they may have overcrowded cities, poorly constructed buildings, and inadequate rescue services.

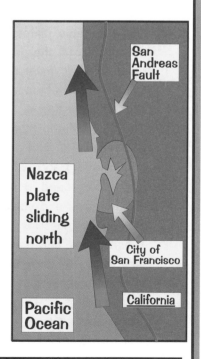

## Learn about Plate Tectonics — but don't get carried away...

There's some more stuff on what happens at plate boundaries on the next page, so make sure all of this is firmly implanted in your brain. You should definitely make sure you know what happens when plates slide past each other, and what is done to cut down on the damage caused. Sounds perfect for a mini-essay — try to remember as many facts as you can, and then see how many you can write down. Scribble and learn.

# Plate Boundaries

*Earth Waves*

## Oceanic and Continental Plates Colliding: The Andes

1) The heavier <u>oceanic</u> plate is always forced <u>underneath</u> the lighter continental plate.

2) This is called a <u>subduction zone</u>.

3) As the oceanic plate is pushed down, parts of it <u>melt</u>. The magma is <u>less dense</u> than the surrounding rock so it <u>rises</u>.

4) Some <u>molten rock</u> finds its way to the surface and <u>volcanoes</u> form, some cools slowly <u>underground</u>.

5) There are also <u>earthquakes</u> as the two plates slowly <u>grind</u> past each other.

6) A deep <u>trench</u> forms on the ocean floor where the <u>oceanic plate</u> is being <u>forced</u> down.

7) The <u>continental</u> crust <u>crumples</u> and <u>folds</u> forming <u>mountains</u> at the coast.

8) The classic example of all this is the west coast of <u>South America</u> where the <u>Andes mountains</u> are. That region has <u>all</u> the features:

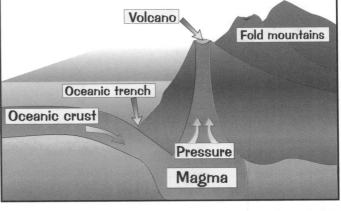

## <u>Volcanoes</u>, <u>earthquakes</u>, an <u>oceanic trench</u> and <u>mountains</u>.

## Sea Floor Spreading — The mid-Atlantic Ridge

1) When tectonic plates move apart, <u>magma</u> rises up to fill the gap and produces <u>new crust</u> (rocks) made of <u>basalt</u> (of course). Sometimes it comes out with great <u>force</u> producing <u>undersea volcanoes</u>.

2) The <u>Mid-Atlantic ridge</u> runs the whole length of the Atlantic and actually cuts through the middle of <u>Iceland</u>, which is why they have <u>hot</u> underground water.

3) Earthquakes and volcanoes under the sea can cause massive <u>tidal waves</u> (tsunami). These waves can cause great destruction when they reach land.

4) As the magma rises up through the gap it forms <u>ridges</u> and <u>underwater mountains</u>.

5) These form a <u>symmetrical pattern</u> either side of the ridge, providing strong <u>evidence</u> for the theory of <u>continental drift</u>.

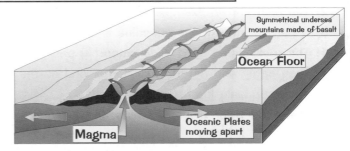

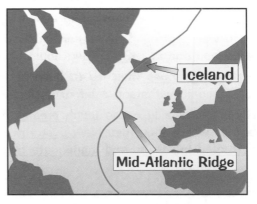

## Another page to learn — don't make a mountain out of it...

That's all that you need to know about <u>plate boundaries</u>, but you do need to know it. Make sure you know how <u>plates meet</u>, and what <u>happens</u> in each case. Most importantly learn <u>why</u> these different cases occur. <u>Mini-essays</u> are the best way to tackle this — <u>learn</u> as many of the details as you can, and then write the essay. <u>Keep going</u> until you've memorised it all.

# Radioactivity

## Radioactive decay is a Random Process

Unstable nuclei decay by emitting radiation — this can be either alpha, beta or gamma radiation, or a combination. The atoms decay at <u>random</u>, so you can't say when any atom will decay. Each nucleus will just decay quite <u>spontaneously</u> in its <u>own good time</u> — it's unaffected by <u>physical</u> conditions like <u>temperature</u> or by any sort of <u>chemical bonding</u> etc.

| Alpha decay | | α-particle |
|---|---|---|
| Uranium-238 | Thorium-234 | γ-ray |
| Carbon-14 | Beta decay | Nitrogen-14 + β-particle |

By decaying, the <u>nucleus</u> will often <u>change</u> into a <u>new element</u>, as shown above.

## Radioactivity is Measured in Becquerels, Bq

The <u>unit</u> used for measuring <u>radioactivity</u> is the <u>Becquerel</u> (Bq). <u>One Becquerel</u> is <u>one nucleus decaying per second</u>. So a count rate of <u>60 counts per minute (60 CPM)</u> would represent <u>1 Bq</u>.

In fact it's a bit tricky to measure exactly how strong a radioactive source is, because the reading you get depends on how close you are to the source. A reading in Becquerels only gives you a sort of vague relative measure of how much radioactivity there is around. Anyway, as long as you know that <u>one Becquerel</u> means <u>one nucleus decaying per second</u> (on average), then you'll be OK in the Exam.

## The Radioactivity of a Sample Decreases Over Time

1) This is <u>pretty obvious</u> when you think about it. Each time a <u>decay</u> happens and an alpha, beta or gamma is given out, it means one more <u>radioactive nucleus</u> has <u>disappeared</u>.

2) Obviously, as the <u>unstable nuclei</u> all steadily disappear, the <u>activity as a whole</u> will also <u>decrease</u>. So the <u>older</u> a sample becomes, the <u>less radiation</u> it will emit.

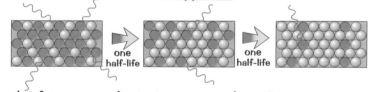

3) <u>How quickly</u> the activity <u>drops off</u> varies a lot from one radio-isotope to another. For <u>some</u> it can take <u>just a few hours</u> whilst others can last for <u>millions of years</u>.

4) The problem with trying to <u>measure</u> this is that <u>the activity never reaches ZERO</u>, which is why we have to use the idea of <u>HALF-LIFE</u> to measure how quickly the activity <u>drops off</u>.

5) Learn this <u>important definition</u> of <u>half-life</u>:

### HALF-LIFE is the TIME TAKEN for HALF of the radioactive atoms now present to DECAY

Another definition of half-life — "<u>The time taken for the activity (or count rate) to fall by half</u>". Use either.

6) A <u>short half-life</u> means the <u>activity falls quickly</u>, because <u>lots</u> of the nuclei decay <u>quickly</u>.

7) A <u>long half-life</u> means the activity <u>falls more slowly</u> because <u>most</u> of the nuclei don't decay <u>for a long time</u> — they just sit there, <u>basically unstable</u>, but kind of <u>biding their time</u>.

Waste from <u>nuclear power plants</u> has a <u>long half life</u>, and needs to be stored for <u>many years</u> before it reaches a safe level. The waste is either stored in <u>cooled tanks</u> or <u>stainless steel containers</u>.

## Definition of Half-life — a freshly woken teenager...

A lot of details on this page — but it's the <u>half-life</u> thing that might take a bit of getting your head round. Read all the stuff, then write it down. And if you make any mistakes, do it <u>again</u>.

# Radioactive Half-life

*Using Half-life*

## Half-life Calculations

The basic idea of half-life is maybe a little confusing, but Exam calculations are pretty straightforward so long as you do them slowly, STEP BY STEP. Like this one:

Example: The activity of a radio-isotope is 640cpm (counts per minute). Two hours later it has fallen to 40 counts per minute. Find the half life of the sample.

Answer: You must go through it in SHORT SIMPLE STEPS like this:

| INITIAL count: | after ONE half-life: | after TWO half-lives: | after THREE half-lives: | after FOUR half-lives: |
|---|---|---|---|---|
| | $(\div 2)\rightarrow$ | $(\div 2)\rightarrow$ | $(\div 2)\rightarrow$ | $(\div 2)\rightarrow$ |
| 640 | 320 | 160 | 80 | 40 |

Notice the careful step by step method, which tells us it takes four half lives for the activity to fall from 640 to 40. Hence two hours represents four half-lives so the half-life is 30 minutes.

## Carbon-14 Calculations — or Radio-Carbon Dating

Carbon-14 makes up about 1/10 000 000 (one ten-millionth) of the carbon in the air. This level stays fairly constant in the atmosphere. The same proportion of C-14 is also found in living things. However, when they die, the C-14 is trapped inside the wood or wool or whatever, and it gradually decays with a half-life of 5,600 years.

By simply measuring the proportion of C-14 found in some old axe handle, burial shroud, etc you can easily calculate how long ago the item was living material using the known half-life.

EXAMPLE: An axe handle was found to contain 1 part in 40 000 000 Carbon-14. Calculate the age of the axe.

ANSWER: The C-14 was originally 1 part in 10 000 000. After one half-life it would be down to 1 part in 20 000 000. After two half-lives it would be down to 1 part in 40 000 000. Hence the axe handle is two C-14 half-lives old, i.e. 2 × 5,600 = 11,200 YEARS OLD.

Note the same old stepwise method, going down one half-life at a time.

## Radioactive Dating of Rocks and Archaeological Specimens

1) The discovery of radioactivity and the idea of half-life gave scientists their first opportunity to accurately work out the age of rocks and fossils and archaeological specimens.

2) By measuring the amount of a radioactive isotope left in a sample, and knowing its half-life, you can work out how long the thing has been around.

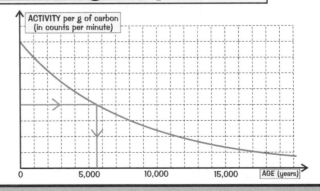

## Learn about Half-life — and get things in proportion...

Half-life and radioactive dating — it's quite a tough topic, but once you've got your head round it it's not too bad. Learn the facts about radioactive dating and work through the examples I've given you. The same goes for calculating the half life of a source — understand the basic theory and then work through the top example till you've got it...

# Revision Summary for Module 11

*More jolly questions which I know you're going to really enjoy. There are lots of bits and bobs on forces and motion which you definitely need to know. Some bits are certainly quite tricky to understand, but there's also loads of straightforward stuff which just need to be learnt, ready for instant regurgitation in the Exam. You have to practise these questions over and over and over again, until you can answer them all really easily — phew, such jolly fun.*

1) What's the difference between speed and velocity? Give an example of each.
2) Write down the formula for working out speed. Find the speed of a partly chewed mouse which hobbles 3.15m in 35s. Find how far he would get in 25 minutes.
3) What's acceleration? Is it the same thing as speed or velocity? What are the units of it?
4) Write down the formula for acceleration.
   What's the acceleration of a soggy pea, flicked from rest to a speed of 14 m/s in 0.4s?
5) Sketch a typical distance-time graph and point out all the important parts of it.
6) Sketch a typical speed-time graph and point out all the important parts of it.
7) Write down six important points relating to each of these graphs.
8) Explain how to calculate velocity from a distance-time graph.
9) Explain how to find speed, distance and acceleration from a velocity-time graph.
10) What are the two different parts of the overall stopping distance of a car?
11) List the three or four factors which affect each of the two parts of stopping distance.
12) Write down the First Law of Motion. Illustrate with a diagram.
13) Write down the Second Law of Motion. Illustrate with a diagram. What's the formula for it?
14) Explain what "resultant force" is. Illustrate with a diagram. When do you most need it?
15) A force of 30N pushes on a trolley of mass 4kg. What will be its acceleration?
16) What's the mass of a cat which accelerates at 8 m/s$^2$ when acted on by a force of 56N?
17) Write down the Third Law of Motion. Illustrate it with four diagrams.
18) Explain what <u>reaction force</u> is and where it pops up. Is it important to know about it?
19) What is gravity? List the two main effects that gravity produces.
20) Explain the difference between mass and weight. What units are they measured in?
21) What's the formula for weight? Illustrate it with a worked example of your own.
22) What is "terminal velocity"?
23) What's the connection between "work done" and "energy transferred"?
24) What's the formula for work done? A crazy dog drags a big branch 12m over the next-door neighbour's front lawn, pulling with a force of 535N. How much energy was transferred?
25) What's the formula for power? What are the units for power?
   Calculate the power output of a motor transferring 3.4kJ of useful energy in 12 minutes.
26) Write down the formulae for calculating kinetic energy and potential energy.
   Calculate the kinetic energy of a milk lorry of mass 4530kg travelling at 21m/s.
27) What causes seismic waves? Sketch diagrams showing the paths of both types, and explain.
28) What are the three different ways that tectonic plates interact at boundaries?
29) What happens when an oceanic plate and a continental plate collide? Draw a diagram.
30) What features does it produce? Which part of the world is the classic example of this?
31) Give the proper definition of radioactive half-life. How long and how short can half-lives be?
32) An old bit of cloth was found to have 1 atom of C-14 to 80 000 000 atoms of C-12.
   Using the information on P.78, calculate the age of the bit of cloth.

*Charge and Energy*

# Static Electricity

Static electricity is all about charges which are <u>not</u> free to move (hence the name). This causes them to build up in one place and it often ends with a <u>spark</u> or a <u>shock</u> when they do finally move.

## 1) Build up of Static is Caused by Friction

1) When two <u>insulating</u> materials are <u>rubbed</u> together, electrons will be <u>scraped off one</u> and <u>dumped</u> on the other.

2) This'll leave a <u>positive</u> static charge on one and a <u>negative</u> static charge on the other.

3) <u>Which way</u> the electrons are transferred <u>depends</u> on the <u>two materials</u> involved.

4) Electrically charged objects <u>attract</u> small objects placed near them.
(Try this: rub a balloon on a woolly "pully", then put it near tiddly bits of paper and watch them jump.)

5) The classic examples are <u>polythene</u> and <u>acetate</u> rods being rubbed with a <u>cloth duster</u>, as shown in the diagrams:

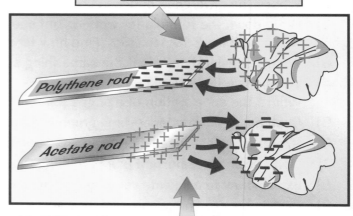

With the <u>polythene rod</u>, electrons move <u>from the duster</u> to the rod.

With the <u>acetate rod</u>, electrons move <u>from the rod</u> to the duster.

## 2) Only Electrons Move — Never the Positive Charges

<u>Watch out for this in Exams</u>. Both positive and negative electrostatic charges are only ever produced by the movement of <u>electrons</u>. The positive charges <u>definitely do not move</u>. A positive static charge is always caused by electrons <u>moving</u> away elsewhere, as shown above.

## 3) Earthing Removes Excess Charge

1) A charged conductor can be <u>discharged safely</u> by connecting it to earth with a <u>metal strap</u>.
2) Electrons flow <u>down</u> the strap to the ground if the charge is <u>negative</u> and flow <u>up</u> the strap from the ground if the charge is <u>positive</u>.
3) Electrons will flow until the <u>excess charge</u> has been <u>removed</u>.

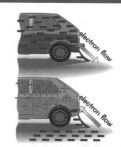

*Higher*

## 4) Like Charges Repel, Opposite Charges Attract

This is <u>easy</u> and, I'd have thought, <u>kind of obvious</u>.
1) Two things with <u>opposite</u> electric charges are <u>attracted</u> to each other.
2) Two things with the <u>same</u> electric charge will <u>repel</u> each other.
3) These forces get <u>weaker</u> the <u>further apart</u> the two things are.

## Phew — it's enough to make your hair stand on end...

The <u>best</u> way to tackle this page is to learn the <u>four</u> headings till you can <u>scribble</u> them all down. Then learn the <u>details</u> for each of the headings — when you think you've got all of them firmly in your head, <u>cover the page</u> and practise <u>scribbling</u> down each heading with all of the details you can remember. <u>Keep trying</u> until you're sure you've got it all...

# Static Electricity

## Static Electricity Being Helpful:

### 1) Inkjet Printer:

1) Tiny droplets of ink are forced out of a fine nozzle, making them electrically charged.
2) The droplets are deflected as they pass between two metal plates. A voltage is applied to the plates — one is negative and the other is positive.
3) The droplets are attracted to the plate of the opposite charge and repelled from the plate with the same charge.

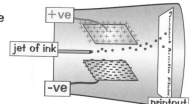

jet of ink
+ve
-ve
printout

4) The size and direction of the voltage across each plate changes so each droplet is deflected to hit a different place on the paper.
5) Lots of tiny dots make up your print-out. Clever.

### 2) Photocopier:

1) A metal plate is electrically charged, and an image of what you're copying is projected onto it.
2) Whiter bits of the thing you're copying make light fall on the plate and the charge leaks away.

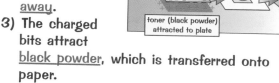

light
-ve
heated rollers
toner (black powder) attracted to plate

3) The charged bits attract black powder, which is transferred onto paper.
4) The paper is heated so the powder sticks.
5) Voilà, a photocopy of your piece of paper (or whatever else you've shoved in there).

Two other applications of static electricity are spray painting of cars and removal of dust from factory chimneys. They might ask you to mention those, but photocopiers and inkjet printers are what they'll be most interested in.

## Static Electricity Being a Little Joker:

### 1) Car Shocks

Air rushing past your car can give it a +ve charge. When you get out and touch the door it gives you a real buzz — in the Exam make sure you say "electrons flow from earth, through you, to neutralise the +ve charge on the car". Some cars have conducting rubber strips which hang down behind the car. This gives a safe discharge to earth, but spoils all the fun.

### 2) Clothing Crackles

When synthetic clothes are dragged over each other (like in a tumble drier) or over your head, electrons get scraped off, leaving static charges on both parts, and that leads to the inevitable — attraction (they stick together) and little sparks / shocks as the charges rearrange themselves.

## Static Electricity Playing at Terrorist:

### 1) Lightning

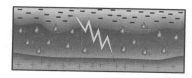

Rain droplets fall to Earth with positive charge. This creates a huge voltage and a big spark.

### 2) Grain Shoots, Paper Rollers and The Fuel Filling Nightmare

grain shoot
paper rollers
fuel tank

1) As fuel flows out of a filler pipe, or paper drags over rollers, or grain shoots out of pipes, static can build up.
2) This can easily lead to a spark and in dusty or fumy places — BOOM!
3) The solution — make the nozzles or rollers out of metal so that the charge is conducted away, instead of building up.
4) It's also good to have earthing straps between the fuel tank and the fuel pipe.

## Static Electricity — learn the shocking truth...

You really need to learn those two big examples at the top. The syllabus mentions photocopiers and inkjet printers so there's bound to be a question. Learn it all and you're laughing.

# Electrical Current

**Charge and Energy**

## In <u>Metals</u> the <u>Current</u> is Carried by <u>Electrons</u>

1) Electric current will only flow if there are <u>charges</u> which can <u>move freely</u>.
2) Metals contain a <u>"sea" of free electrons</u> (which are <u>negatively</u> charged) and which <u>flow throughout the metal</u>.
3) This is what allows <u>electric current</u> to flow so well <u>in all metals</u>.

## In <u>Electrolytes</u>, <u>Current</u> is Carried by Both +ve and −ve Charges

1) <u>Electrolytes</u> are <u>liquids</u> containing charges which can <u>move freely</u>.
2) They are either <u>ions dissolved in water</u>, like salt solution, or <u>molten ionic liquids</u>, like molten sodium chloride.
3) When a voltage is applied, the <u>positive</u> ions move towards the <u>−ve</u>, and the <u>negative</u> ions move towards the <u>+ve</u>. This is an <u>electric current</u>.

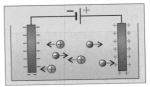

## Calculating <u>Electrical Power</u>

1) The standard formula for <u>electrical power</u> is <u>$P = I \times V$</u>.
2) <u>Power</u> is measured in <u>Watts</u>, <u>Voltage</u> in <u>Volts</u>, and <u>Current</u> in <u>Amps</u>.
3) Most electrical goods indicate their <u>power rating</u> and <u>voltage rating</u>.
   To work out the <u>current</u> that will normally flow use '<u>$P = I \times V$</u>', or rather, '<u>$I = P/V$</u>'.
   <u>Example</u>: *A hairdrier is rated at 240V, 1.1kW. Find the current which flows.*
   <u>ANSWER</u>: $I = P/V = 1100/240 = 4.6A$.

## Electrical <u>Charge and Energy Change</u>

1) Current is the <u>flow of electrical charge</u> around a circuit. When <u>current</u> (I) flows past a point in a circuit for a length of <u>time</u> (t) then a certain amount of <u>charge</u> (Q) will pass. This is given by the formula: <u>$Q = I \times t$</u>.
   <u>More charge</u> passes around the circuit when a <u>bigger current</u> flows.

2) When electrical <u>charge</u> (Q) goes through a <u>change in voltage</u> (V), <u>energy</u> (E) is <u>transferred</u>. Energy is <u>supplied to the charge</u> at the <u>power source</u> to raise it through a voltage. The charge <u>gives up</u> this energy when it <u>falls through any voltage drop</u> in <u>components</u> elsewhere in the circuit. The formula is real simple: <u>$E = I \times V \times t$</u>.

3) The <u>bigger</u> the <u>change in voltage</u> (or potential difference), the <u>more energy</u> is transferred for a <u>given amount of charge</u> passing through the circuit. That means that a battery with a <u>bigger voltage</u> will supply <u>more energy</u> to the circuit for <u>every Coulomb of charge</u> which flows round it, because the charge is raised up "<u>higher</u>" at the start — and as the diagram shows, <u>more energy will be dissipated</u> in the circuit too. This gives rise to <u>two definitions</u> which I guess you should learn, although they're seriously dull:

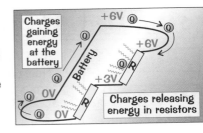

1) <u>ONE VOLT</u> is <u>ONE JOULE PER COULOMB</u>
2) <u>VOLTAGE</u> is the <u>ENERGY TRANSFERRED PER UNIT CHARGE</u> passed

## *Electricity — why does it all turn out so dreary...*

I try to make it interesting, really I do. I mean, underneath it all, electricity is pretty good stuff, but somehow every page just seems to end up stuffed full of interminably dreary facts. Well look, I tried, OK. It may be dreary but you've just gotta <u>learn it all</u>, and that's that.

# Magnetic Fields

*Charge and Energy*

There's a proper definition of a <u>magnetic field</u> which you really ought to learn:

> A <u>MAGNETIC FIELD</u> is a region where <u>MAGNETIC MATERIALS</u> (like iron and steel) and also <u>WIRES CARRYING CURRENTS</u> experience <u>A FORCE</u> acting on them.

## Learn all These *Magnetic Field Diagrams*, *Arrow-perfect*

They're real likely to give you one of these diagrams to do in your Exam.
So make sure you know them, especially <u>which way the arrows point</u> — ALWAYS from N to S!

### Bar Magnet

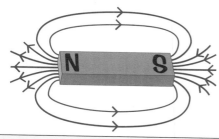

### Solenoid

Same field as a bar magnet <u>outside</u>.

<u>Strong</u> and <u>uniform</u> field on the <u>inside</u>.

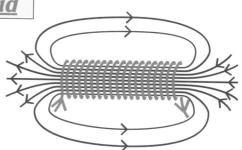

### Two Bar Magnets *Attracting*

Opposite poles ATTRACT, as I'm sure you know.

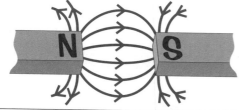

### Two Bar Magnets *Repelling*

Like poles REPEL, as you must surely know.

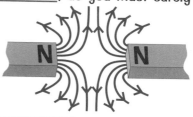

### The Earth's Magnetic Field

Note that the <u>magnetic poles</u> are <u>opposite</u> to the <u>Geographic Poles</u>, ie. the South Pole is at the North Pole — if you see what I mean!

### The Magnetic Field Round a Current-carrying Wire

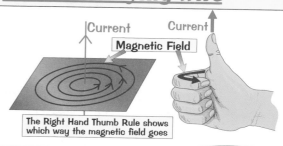

Current

Current

Magnetic Field

The Right Hand Thumb Rule shows which way the magnetic field goes

## A *Plotting Compass* *is a* *Freely Suspended Magnet*

1) This means it always <u>aligns itself</u> with the <u>magnetic field</u> that it's in.
2) This is great for plotting <u>magnetic field lines</u> like around the <u>bar magnets</u> shown above.
3) Away from any magnets, it will <u>align</u> with the magnetic field of the <u>Earth</u> and point <u>North</u>.
4) <u>Any magnet</u> suspended so it can turn <u>freely</u> will also come to rest pointing <u>North-South</u>.
5) The end of the magnet which points North is called a "<u>North-seeking pole</u>" or "<u>magnetic North</u>". The end pointing South will therefore be a "<u>magnetic South pole</u>". This is how they got their names.

## Magnetic fields — there's no getting away from them...

Mmm, this is a nice easy page for you isn't it. Learn the definition of what a magnetic field is and the six field diagrams. Also learn those five details about plotting compasses and which way the poles are compared to the Earth. Then <u>cover the page</u> and <u>scribble it all down</u>.

**Charge and Energy**

# The Motor Effect

Anything carrying a current in a magnetic field will experience a force.

## A Current in a Magnetic Field Experiences a Force

The diagrams below demonstrate the force on a current-carrying wire placed in a magnetic field.
The force gets bigger if either the current or the magnetic field is made bigger.

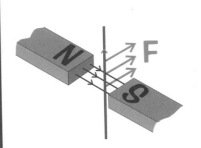

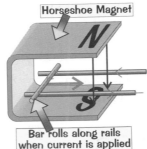

Horseshoe Magnet

Bar rolls along rails when current is applied

1) Note that in both cases the force on the wire is at 90° to the wire and to the magnetic field.
2) You can always predict which way the force will act using Fleming's LHR as shown below.
3) To experience the full force, the wire has to be at 90° to the magnetic field.
4) The direction of the force is reversed if either:
   a) the direction of the current is reversed.
   b) the direction of the magnetic field is reversed.

**The SIZE of the Force Increases if you:**
1) Increase the strength of the MAGNETIC FIELD
2) Increase the size of the CURRENT

## The Simple DC Electric Motor

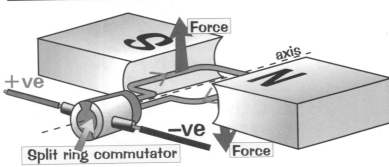

Force

axis

+ve

−ve

Force

Split ring commutator

**4 Factors which Speed it up**
1) More CURRENT
2) More TURNS on the coil
3) STRONGER MAGNETIC FIELD
4) A SOFT IRON CORE in the coil

1) The diagram shows the forces acting on the two side arms of the coil.
2) These forces are just the usual forces which act on any current in a magnetic field.
3) Because the coil is on a spindle and the forces act one up and one down, it rotates.
4) The split ring commutator is a clever way of "swapping the contacts every half turn to keep the motor rotating in the same direction". Learn that statement because they might ask you.
5) The direction of the motor can be reversed either by swapping the polarity of the DC supply or swapping the magnetic poles over.

### Fleming's Left Hand Rule tells you Which way the Force Acts

1) They could test if you can do this, so practise.
2) Using your left hand, point your First finger in the direction of the Field and your seCond finger in the direction of the Current.
3) Your thumb will then point in the direction of the force (motion).

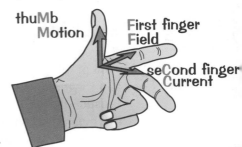

thuMb Motion

First finger Field

seCond finger Current

## Fleming! — how many broken wrists has he caused already...

Same old routine here. Learn all the details, diagrams and all, then cover the page and scribble it all down again from memory. I presume you do realise that you should be scribbling it down as scruffy as you like — because all you're trying to do is make sure that you really do know it.

# Transformers

What transformers actually *do* is <u>really simple</u> — they make a voltage bigger or smaller. Make sure you learn <u>what they look like</u> and <u>what they do</u> first, then worry about <u>how</u> they actually do it.

## Transformers *Change the Voltage* — *but only AC*

1) Transformers <u>convert</u> an alternating voltage into a <u>bigger or smaller</u> alternating voltage. (By the way, "alternating voltage" goes hand in hand with Alternating Current, AC).
2) For example, you could put <u>240V</u> (AC) into a transformer and get, say <u>20V</u> (AC) out of it.
3) The precise change in the voltage is determined by the <u>number of turns</u> on the two coils on the transformer (known as the <u>Primary Coil</u> and the <u>Secondary Coil</u> ).

## Transformers *have* Two Coils *and an* Iron core

You need to know the <u>construction</u> of transformers, so learn this diagram:

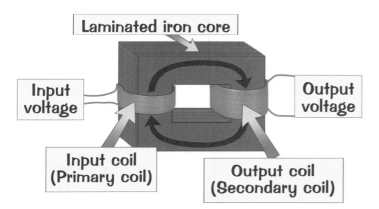

Laminated iron core

Input voltage

Output voltage

Input coil (Primary coil)

Output coil (Secondary coil)

The <u>SIMPLE RULE</u> for the <u>VOLTAGES</u>:

1) If the <u>output coil</u> has, say, <u>twice as many turns</u> of wire as the input coil, then the <u>output voltage</u> will be <u>twice as big</u> as the input voltage.
2) Alternatively, if the output coil has, say, a ¼ <u>the number of turns</u> of the input coil, then it will have ¼ <u>the voltage</u> too. It's dead easy really.

### A *"Step-Up"* or *"Step-Down"* *in Voltage depends on the* Coils

In a <u>step-up transformer</u>, the <u>output voltage</u> is <u>bigger</u> — there are *more* turns on the secondary coil.
In a <u>step-down transformer</u>, the <u>output voltage</u> is <u>smaller</u> — there are <u>fewer turns</u> on the secondary.

## Transformers *work using* Electromagnetic Induction

"Electromagnetic Induction" is a really difficult area of physics and the Edexcel Syllabus seems to skirt around it quite nicely, which is <u>good news</u> for you. This is the definition of it:

*ELECTROMAGNETIC INDUCTION*: The creation of a *VOLTAGE* (and maybe current) in a wire which is experiencing a *CHANGE IN MAGNETIC FIELD*.

1) <u>Electromagnetic Induction</u> is the principle which makes transformers work.
2) The <u>AC voltage</u> in the primary coil creates a "<u>constantly changing magnetic field</u>" inside the iron core.
3) This in turn creates a *new AC voltage* (and current) inside the secondary coil.   Simple?   Not really.

Electromagnetic Induction is also the principle which generates all our electricity in power stations.

## Transformers — *they change alternating voltages...*

Transformers might seem scary at first, but there really isn't that much to know. This page has four sections with a few details in each. All you have to do is learn the headings, then the details. Then it's the same old thing: <u>Cover</u> the page and <u>scribble down</u> what you know. Then <u>try again</u>.

> Charge and Energy

# Power Transmission

Step-up and step-down transformers are <u>essential</u> for the efficient <u>transmission</u> of electricity.

## Pylon Cables are at 400,000 V to keep the Current Low

The <u>National Grid</u> is the network of <u>pylons and cables</u>, covering the whole country, which <u>transmits electricity</u> from the power stations to homes and industry.

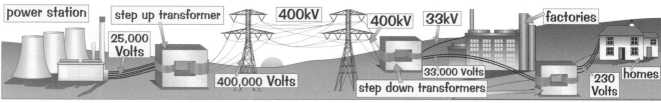

The <u>trickiest bits</u> you'll need to <u>fully understand</u> are: Why is the <u>voltage</u> on pylon cables so <u>high</u> (400 000V), and why does it have to be <u>AC</u> rather than <u>DC</u>. The numbered points below will explain it.

1) The formula for <u>power supplied</u> is: <u>Power = Voltage × Current</u> or: <u>P = V×I</u>.
2) So to transmit <u>a lot of power</u>, you either need <u>high voltage</u> or <u>high current</u>.
3) The problem with <u>high current</u> is the <u>loss</u> (as heat) due to the <u>resistance</u> of the cables.
4) It's much <u>cheaper</u> to boost the voltage up to <u>400,000V</u> and keep the current <u>very low</u>.
5) This requires <u>transformers</u>, as well as <u>big pylons</u> with <u>huge insulators</u>, but it's still <u>cheaper</u>.
6) The transformers have to <u>step</u> the voltage <u>up</u> at one end, for <u>efficient transmission</u>, and then bring it back down to <u>safe useable levels</u> at the other end.
7) This is why it has to be <u>AC</u> on the National Grid — so that the <u>transformers</u> will work!

## The Transformer Equation — use it Either Way Up

In words: The <u>ratio of turns</u> on the two coils equals the <u>ratio of their voltages</u>.

$$\frac{\text{Primary Voltage}}{\text{Secondary Voltage}} = \frac{\text{Number of turns on Primary}}{\text{Number of turns on Secondary}}$$

$$\frac{V_P}{V_S} = \frac{N_P}{N_S}$$
or
$$\frac{V_S}{V_P} = \frac{N_S}{N_P}$$

Well, it's <u>just another formula</u>. You stick in the numbers <u>you've got</u> and work out the one <u>that's left</u>. It's real useful to remember you can write it <u>either way up</u> — these examples are much trickier algebra-wise if you start with $V_S$ on the bottom...

**Example** A transformer has 40 turns on the primary and 800 on the secondary. If the input voltage is 1000V find the output voltage.

ANSWER: $V_S/V_P = N_S/N_P$ so $V_S/1000 = 800/40$ $V_S = 1000×(800/40) = \underline{20,000V}$

**Example** A transformer has a primary voltage of 800V and a secondary voltage of 20V. If there are 1200 turns on the primary, find the number of secondary turns.

ANSWER: $V_S/V_P = N_S/N_P$ so $20/800 = N_S/1200$ $N_S = 1200×(20/800) = \underline{30\text{ turns}}$

## Step up, step down — sounds like hard work...

Quite a few tricky details on this page. The <u>transformer</u> calculations are easy enough once you know the formula, so get some marks in the bag now and <u>learn it</u>. Fully explaining why pylon cables are at <u>400,000V</u> is actually a bit trickier — but you need to learn it. Keep going until you can remember it <u>quickly</u> and <u>easily</u> from memory...

# *Waves*

Waves look really complicated, but there's only a few <u>key facts</u> you really need to know...

## *All Waves Carry Energy — Without Transferring Matter*

1) <u>Light</u>, <u>infrared</u>, and <u>microwaves</u> all make things <u>heat up</u>. <u>X-rays</u> and <u>gamma rays</u> can cause <u>ionisation</u> and <u>damage</u> to cells, which also shows that they carry <u>energy</u>.

2) <u>Loud</u> sounds make things <u>vibrate or move</u>. Even really <u>quiet</u> sounds move your <u>ear drum</u>.

3) Waves on the sea can <u>toss big boats</u> around and can generate <u>electricity</u>.

## *Two Important Wave Speed Formulae for you to Learn*

They're just formulae, <u>just like all the other formulae</u>, and the <u>same old rules apply</u>.
Mind you, there are two of them, so that means you need to learn when to use each one.

> Wave Speed (m/s) = Distance (m) / Time (s)

> Wave Speed (m/s) = Frequency (Hz) x Wavelength (m)

## *The First Rule: Try and Choose the Right Formula*

1) People have way too much <u>difficulty</u> deciding which <u>formula</u> to use.

2) All too often the question starts with "*A wave is travelling...*", and in they leap with "$v = f\lambda$".

3) To choose the <u>right</u> formula you have to look for the <u>three</u> quantities mentioned in the question.

4) If the question mentions <u>speed</u>, <u>frequency</u> and <u>wavelength</u> then sure, "$v = f\lambda$" is the one to use.

5) But if it has <u>speed</u>, <u>time</u> and <u>distance</u> then "$s = d/t$" is more the order of the day.

## *Example — Water Ripples*

a) Some ripples travel 55cm in 5 seconds. Find their speed in cm/s.
<u>Answer</u>: Speed, distance and time are mentioned, so use "$s = d/t$":  $s = d/t = 55/5 = \underline{11 \text{ cm/s}}$

b) The wavelength of these waves is found to be 2.2cm. What is their frequency?
<u>Answer</u>: This time we have f and $\lambda$ mentioned, so we use "$v = f\lambda$", which tells us that
$f = v/\lambda = 11\text{cm/s} \div 2.2\text{cm} = \underline{5\text{Hz}}$  (It's very cool to use cm/s with cm, s and Hz)

## *Digital Signals are Far Better Quality than Analogue*

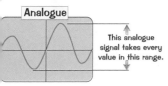
This analogue signal takes every value in this range.

An <u>analogue</u> wave can take <u>any</u> value within a certain range. (Remember: <u>an</u>alogue — <u>any</u>.) A <u>digital</u> signal on the other hand can only take <u>two</u> values — <u>on</u> or <u>off</u>.

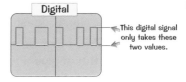
This digital signal only takes these two values.

<u>Digital</u> and <u>Analogue</u> waves can both <u>transmit information</u>. You need to know these <u>two differences</u>:

1) When a digital signal is transmitted, it remains exactly the <u>same</u> as the original. Any noise picked up is removed, which makes them <u>higher quality</u> than analogue.

2) <u>Loads more information</u> can be sent as digital signals compared to analogue (in a certain time). Many digital signals can be transmitted at once by a clever way of <u>overlapping</u> them on the <u>same</u> cable or EM wave — but you don't need to learn how they do it. Phew.

## *This stuff on formulae is really painful — I mean it MHz...*

<u>Sift out</u> the main points from this page, <u>cover it up</u> and <u>scribble</u> them down again. Then try this one.
A wave has a frequency of 2500Hz and a wavelength of 13.2cm. Find its speed.

# Total Internal Reflection

**Waves**

All waves have common features — they can be reflected and refracted for instance.

## Total Internal Reflection *and The* Critical Angle

1) <u>Refraction</u> happens when <u>light</u> is <u>coming out</u> of something <u>dense</u> like <u>glass</u> or <u>water</u> or <u>perspex</u>.
2) If the <u>angle</u> is <u>shallow</u> enough the ray <u>won't</u> come out at all, but <u>reflects</u> back into the glass (or whatever). This is called <u>total internal reflection</u> because <u>all</u> of the light <u>reflects back in</u>.
3) You definitely need to learn this set of <u>three diagrams</u> which show the three conditions:

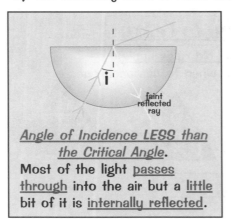 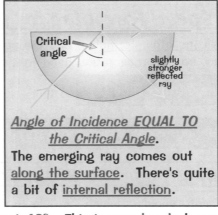 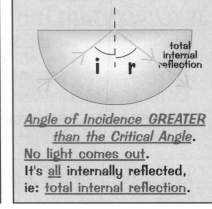

| *Angle of Incidence LESS than the Critical Angle*. | *Angle of Incidence EQUAL TO the Critical Angle*. | *Angle of Incidence GREATER than the Critical Angle*. |
|---|---|---|
| Most of the light <u>passes through</u> into the air but a <u>little</u> bit of it is <u>internally reflected</u>. | The emerging ray comes out <u>along the surface</u>. There's quite a bit of <u>internal reflection</u>. | <u>No light comes out</u>. It's <u>all</u> internally reflected, ie: <u>total internal reflection</u>. |

1) The <u>Critical Angle</u> for <u>glass</u> is about <u>42°</u>. This is <u>very handy</u> because it means <u>45° angles</u> can be used to get <u>total internal reflection</u> as in the <u>prisms</u> in the <u>periscope</u> shown below.
2) In <u>diamond</u> the <u>Critical Angle</u> is much <u>lower</u>, about <u>24°</u>. This is the reason why diamonds <u>sparkle</u> so much, because there are lots of <u>internal reflections</u>.

## Periscopes *often use* Total Internal Reflection

Periscopes use <u>Total Internal Reflection</u> of light in <u>45° prisms</u>. Prisms are used because they give a slightly <u>better reflection</u> than a <u>mirror</u> would and they're also <u>easier</u> to hold accurately <u>in place</u>. They could ask you to <u>complete</u> a diagram of a periscope, and unless you've <u>practised</u> beforehand you'll find it pretty <u>tricky</u> to draw the prisms <u>properly</u>.

## Optical Fibres *— Communications and Endoscopes*

1) <u>Optical fibres</u> can carry <u>information</u> over <u>long distances</u> by repeated <u>total internal reflections</u>.
2) Optical communications have several <u>advantages</u> over <u>electrical signals</u> in wires.
   a) a cable of the <u>same</u> diameter can carry a lot <u>more information</u>.
   b) the signals cannot be <u>tapped</u> into, or suffer <u>interference</u> from electrical sources.
   c) the signal doesn't need <u>boosting</u> as often.
3) The fibre must be <u>narrow</u> enough to keep the angles <u>above</u> the critical angle, as shown, so the fibre mustn't be bent too <u>sharply</u> anywhere.

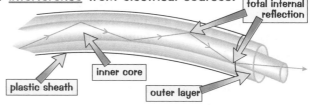

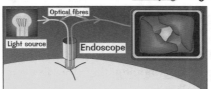

An endoscope is a <u>narrow bunch</u> of <u>optical fibres</u> with a <u>lens system</u> at each end. Another bunch of fibres carries light down <u>inside</u> to see with. The image is displayed as a full colour <u>moving image</u> on a **TV** screen. This means they can do operations <u>without</u> cutting big holes in people.

## *Total Internal Reflection — the only way to a relaxed mind...*

They always have <u>at least one</u> of these applications of total internal reflection in the Exam. <u>Learn them all</u>. None of this is difficult, but just make sure you've got all the details in your head.

# Diffraction

*Waves*

This word sounds a lot more technical than it really is.

## Diffraction _is Just the_ "Spreading Out" _of Waves_

All waves tend to spread out at the edges when they pass through a gap or past an edge (obstacle).  Instead of saying that the wave "spreads out" or "bends" round a corner you should say that it diffracts around the corner.  It's as easy as that.  That's all diffraction means.

## A Wave Spreads More _if it Passes Through a_ Narrow Gap

The ripple tank shows this effect quite nicely.  The same effect applies to light and sound too.

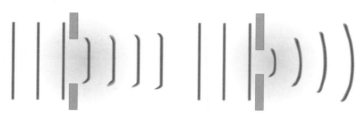

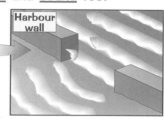

Harbour walls diffract waves in the same way as the ripple tank.

1)  A 'narrow' gap is one which is about the same size as the wavelength or less.
2)  Obviously then, the question of whether a gap is 'narrow' or not depends on the wave in question. What may be a narrow gap for a water wave will be a huge gap for a light wave.
3)  It should be obvious then, that the longer the wavelength of a wave the more it will diffract.

## Sounds Always _Diffract Quite a Lot_, Because λ is Quite Big

1)  Most sounds have wavelengths in air of around 0.1m, which is quite long.
2)  This means they spread out round corners when they pass through doorways or by large buildings, so you can still hear people even when you can't see them (the sound usually reflects off walls too which also helps).
3)  Higher frequency sounds will have shorter wavelengths, so they won't diffract as much, which is why things sound more 'muffled' when you hear them from round corners.

## Long Wavelength Radio Waves Diffract Easily Over Hills _and into_ Buildings

## Visible Light _on the other hand_

has a very short wavelength, and it'll only diffract with a very narrow slit:

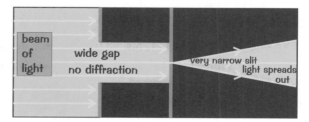

The spreading or diffraction of light and radio waves is good evidence that light is a wave.

## Diffraction — it can drive you round the bend...

People usually don't know much about diffraction, mainly because there are so few lab demos you can do to show it, and there's also very little to say about it — about one page's worth, in fact.  The thing is though, if you just learn this page properly, then you'll know all you need to.

# Forces and Loads

## Hooke's Law — Extension is Proportional to Load

Hooke's Law is <u>seriously easy</u>. It just says:

> If you <u>STRETCH</u> something with a <u>STEADILY INCREASING FORCE</u>, then the <u>LENGTH</u> will <u>INCREASE STEADILY</u> too.

The important thing to measure in a Hooke's Law experiment is not so much the total length as the <u>extension</u>.

> <u>EXTENSION</u> is the <u>INCREASE IN LENGTH</u> compared to the original length with <u>NO FORCE APPLIED</u>.

For most materials, you'll find that the <u>EXTENSION IS PROPORTIONAL TO THE LOAD</u>, which just means if you <u>double</u> the load, the <u>extension is double too</u>.

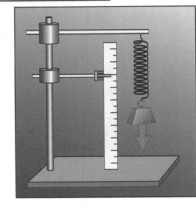

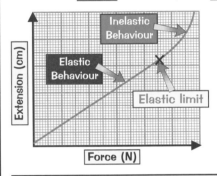

This always gives a <u>STRAIGHT LINE GRAPH THROUGH THE ORIGIN</u>, as shown here for a <u>metal wire</u>. <u>Rubber bands</u> and <u>springs</u> have similar graphs to this.

Notice that there's an <u>ELASTIC LIMIT</u>. For extensions <u>less</u> than this, the wire or spring <u>returns to its original shape</u>, but if stretched <u>beyond</u> the elastic limit, it behaves <u>INELASTICALLY</u>, which means it <u>doesn't</u> follow Hooke's Law and that it also <u>won't return</u> to its original shape.

## Reaction Forces on Beams are biggest near the weight

You need to know about weights on beams — it's fine so long as you remember these <u>important points</u>:

1) The <u>downward force</u> from the weight is balanced by <u>upward forces</u> from the <u>supports</u> at the ends of the beam. If the weight is in the <u>middle</u> of the beam, then the upward forces at each end are <u>equal</u>.

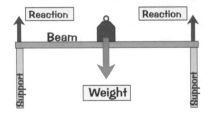

2) The <u>closer</u> the weight is to <u>one end</u>, the larger the "<u>upward reaction force</u>" exerted by the support at <u>that end</u>. If a weight is <u>twice as close</u> to the right end, the right support exerts <u>twice as much force</u> as the left — as shown by the <u>bigger arrow</u>: if <u>three times</u> as close, <u>three times</u> the force, etc.

3) If the weight is at the <u>end</u> of the beam, then the support at that end exerts <u>all</u> of the upward force.

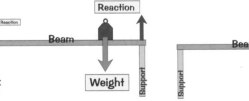

<u>EXAMPLE:</u> A <u>10N</u> weight is placed <u>0.2m</u> from one end of a <u>1 metre</u> long beam. Find the <u>upward force</u> at <u>each end</u>.

<u>ANSWER:</u> With a <u>detailed sketch</u> as shown, we find the <u>other distance = 0.8m</u>. This shows that the downward force of 10N is <u>four times closer to A</u> than B. This means the reaction force must be <u>four times greater at A</u> than at B. Don't forget also that the two upward forces <u>added together</u> must <u>equal</u> the downward force of <u>10N</u>.

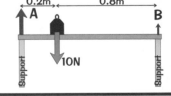

The maths is nice and simple in this example, so it's easy to work out that the two forces must be   A: <u>8N</u>   B: <u>2N</u>

## Hooke's Law — it can stretch you to the limit...

<u>Hooke's Law</u> is just about as easy as it gets, so make sure you know all the little details. Remember the difference between <u>elastic</u> and <u>inelastic</u> stretching and the graph. Then remember the <u>four</u> points on <u>beams</u> and the <u>diagrams</u> that go with them. Come on, <u>cover</u> the page...

# Pressure and Volume

Gas molecules are in <u>constant random motion</u>. They keep <u>bashing</u> into the sides of their container — and this is what creates the <u>pressure</u> of a gas. The more they bash into the sides, the <u>greater</u> the pressure. As you <u>squash</u> a gas down into a <u>smaller</u> volume, the pressure <u>increases</u> because the gas particles are bashing into the walls <u>more often</u>. There's a <u>simple rule</u> for it:

> If you squash a gas into a <u>SMALLER SPACE</u>, the <u>PRESSURE</u> goes up in <u>PROPORTION</u> to how much you squash it. eg. if you squash it to <u>HALF</u> the amount of space, it'll end up at <u>TWICE</u> the pressure it was before (so long as you don't let it get hotter or colder, or let any escape). Simple, innit?

It can work <u>both ways</u> too. If you <u>increase the pressure</u>, the <u>volume must decrease</u>. If you <u>increase the volume</u>, the <u>pressure must decrease</u>. That's all pretty obvious though isn't it?

## Gas Syringe Experiments

1) A <u>gas syringe</u> makes a pretty good <u>airtight seal</u> and is great for demonstrating these rules.
2) You put <u>weights on the top</u> to give a <u>definite</u> known force pushing down on the piston.
3) If you <u>double the weight</u>, you also <u>double the force</u> which <u>doubles the pressure</u>.
4) You can then measure the <u>volume change</u> using the <u>scale</u> on the side of the syringe. Easy peasy.

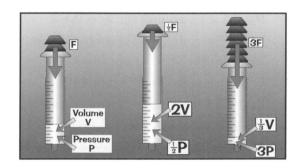

## Using the Formula "PV = Constant" or "$P_1V_1 = P_2V_2$"

Well what can I say, it's another formula. Not one you can put in a triangle, but still the same old idea — <u>stick in the numbers</u> they give you, and <u>work out the value</u> for the remaining letter. Please try and get it into your head that you don't need to <u>fully understand</u> the Physics — you just need some "common sense" about <u>formulae</u>. Understanding always helps, but you can still get the right answer without it! You've just got to identify the values for each letter — the rest is <u>very routine</u>.

<u>EXAMPLE:</u> A gas is compressed from a volume of 300cm³ at a pressure of 2.5 atmospheres down to a volume of 175cm³. Find the new pressure, in atmospheres.

<u>ANSWER:</u> "$P_1V_1 = P_2V_2$" gives $2.5 \times 300 = P_2 \times 175$, so $P_2 = (2.5 \times 300) \div 175 = 4.3$ atm.

NB. For <u>this formula</u>, always keep the units <u>the same</u> as they give them (in this case in <u>atmospheres</u>).

## Kinetic Theory Explains it all Very Nicely

1) The <u>pressure</u> which a gas <u>exerts</u> on the <u>container</u> is caused by the particles whizzing about and <u>bashing into</u> (exerting a force on) <u>the walls</u> of the container. It depends on <u>two things</u> — how <u>fast</u> they're going and <u>how often</u> they hit the walls.

2) <u>How often</u> they hit the walls depends on how <u>squashed up</u> they are. When the <u>volume is reduced</u>, the particles become <u>more squashed up</u> and so they hit the walls <u>more often</u>, and hence the <u>pressure increases</u>. The <u>speed</u> of the particles <u>won't change</u> so long as the <u>temperature</u> doesn't change.

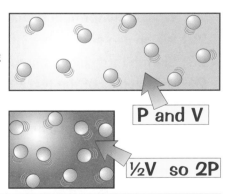

P and V

½V so 2P

## Less space, more collisions, more pressure — just like London...

This is another topic that can seem a lot more confusing than it really is. The basic principle is simple enough, and so is the Gas Syringe demo. The formula might look bad but really there's nothing to it. In the end it's just stuff that needs <u>learning</u>, that's all. <u>Scribble</u>.

# Revision Summary for Module Twelve

*It's an outrage — just so much stuff you've gotta learn — it's all work, work, work, no time to rest, no time to play. But then that's the grim cruel reality of life in modern Britain — just drudgery, hard work and untold weariness... "and then he woke up and it had all been a dream..." Yeah, maybe life's not so bad after all — even for hard-done-to teenagers. Just a few jolly bits and bobs to learn in warm, cosy, comfortable civilisation. Practise these questions over and over again till you can answer them effortlessly. Smile and enjoy.* ☺

1) What is static electricity? What is nearly always the cause of it building up?
2) Which particles move when static builds up, and which ones don't?
3) What is the charge on electrons?
4) How does earthing remove the excess charge on something? What needs to move?
5) Describe in detail how each of these machines use static electricity:
   a) inkjet printer  b) photocopier.
6) Give *one* example of static being:  a) a little joker  b) terrorist.
7) What is the standard formula for calculating electrical power?
8) What is the definition of current?
9) Find the charge passed when a current of 2A flows for 2 minutes.
10) What is the formula relating energy, current, time and voltage?
11) What carries current in metals? What carries current in an electrolyte?
12) Give the proper definition of a magnetic field.
13) Sketch magnetic fields for:  a) a bar magnet,  b) a solenoid,  c) two magnets attracting,
      d) two magnets repelling,  e) the Earth's magnetic field,  f) a current-carrying wire.
14) What's the Right Hand Thumb Rule for?
15) Give a brief description of how a simple DC electric motor works.
16) What do you use Fleming's Left Hand Rule for? What direction do your fingers point in?
17) Sketch the two types of transformer, and highlight the main details. Explain how they work.
18) Why would a transformer not work to step up DC voltages?
20) Explain why the National Grid is at 400 kV.
19) Write down the transformer equation. Do your own worked example — it's good practice.
21) What's the formula relating wave speed, frequency and wavelength?
22) Which can carry more information — Analogue or Digital radio signals?
23) Sketch three diagrams to illustrate Total Internal Reflection and the Critical Angle.
24) Give details of the two main uses of optical fibres. How do optical fibres work?
25) What is diffraction? Sketch the diffraction of  a) water waves  b) sound waves  c) light.
26) Why might a house next to a hill get poor TV reception but good longwave radio reception?
27) What is Hooke's law? Draw a graph showing what happens when a force is applied to a spring.
28) A 5N force is placed 0.1m from one end of a metre long beam.
    Do a sketch and find the upward forces at each end of the beam.
29) How are pressure and volume related for a gas? What needs to be kept constant?
30) Explain how the random movement of gas molecules gives rise to pressure on the walls of
     a container of gas?

# *Index*

# *Index*

# *Index*

# Index

## Numerical answers to questions

**p58 bottom of page** 1) $Fe_2O_3(s) + 3H_2(g) \rightarrow 2Fe(s) + 3H_2O(l)$  2) $6HCl(aq) + 2Al(s) \rightarrow 2AlCl_3(aq)$

**p61 bottom of page** 1) Cu=64 K=30 Kr=84 Fe=56 Cl=35.5  2) NaOH=40 $Fe_2O_3$=160 $C_6H_{14}$=86 $Mg(NO_3)_2$=148

**p62 bottom of page** 1) 21.4g

**p64 revision summary** 18 a) $CaCO_3(s) + 2HCl \rightarrow CaCl_2(aq) + H_2O(l) + CO_2(g)$   b) $Ca(s) + 2H_2O(l) \rightarrow Ca(OH)_2(aq) + H_2(g)$ c) $H_2SO_4(aq) + 2KOH(aq) \rightarrow K_2SO_4(aq) + 2H_2O(l)$   d) $Fe_2O_3(s) \rightarrow 2Fe(s) + H_2O(l)$
24 a) 40  b) 108  c) 44  d) 84  e) 106  f) 81  g) 56  h) 17  i) 58  j) 58.5  k) 127   25) a) 186.8g b) 80.3g c) 20.1 g
27) a) $Fe_2O_3$  b) $CaF_2$  c) $C_5H_{12}$  d) $MgSO_4$

**p79 revision summary** 2) 0.09m/s  135m 4) 35ms$^{-2}$ 15) 7.5ms$^{-2}$ 16) 7kg 24 ) 6420J 25) 4.73W   26) 998 865J 32) 16 800 years

**p92 revision summary** 9) 240C 28) 4.5N at the end nearest the force, 0.5N at the end furthest away.